NOT A PODMATCH MEMBER YET?

PodMatch is the premier site for entrepreneurs, thought leaders and influencers to find some of the world's top podcast shows and be a guest.

With two value-packed membership levels, joining PodMatch is one of the smartest and most cost-effective ways to share your message on other podcast shows.

Joining the PodMatch family is quick and simple. Just visit:

https://podmatch.com/signup/today

PodMatch
Guest
Mastery

**A Guide to Getting Booked on
Successful Podcasts & Sharing
Your Message by Learning From
Top PodMatch Guest Members**

PODCAST GUESTS LOVE PODMATCH!

PodMatch is a simple way to find guests AND be a guest! I've met some amazing people, had rich conversations, and grown my audience and podcast downloads. What a serendipity!

—Andrea Johnson

PodMatch is a resourceful, respectful community of professionals with one goal in mind - to connect with others to share insightful conversations with audiences all over the world. Kudos to PodMatch and their founders for providing such an excellent Podcast watering hole!

—Jennifer Maurer

PodMatch is a no-brainer for finding the best guests for my podcast, and the best podcasts for me to be a guest on as well! I can't believe I fumbled my way through outreach and filtering incoming requests before I found PodMatch. There's no going back for me!

—John Meese

PodMatch has been a godsend to me. It solved problem I have been wanting to solve for a long time, namely. how to get a lot of great shows at a bargain price.

—Nicky Billou

I appreciate PodMatch so much. I am getting so much out of being a guest, and the platform is amazing!

—Karyn Seitz

I'm a latecomer to the world of podcasting, and PodMatch enabled me to play catch-up big time. I've only been a PodMatch member for a month, and I've already been a guest on several excellent shows and have over dozen more either scheduled or in the works. PodMatch made this quick and easy. That's important, since as a book author, public speaker, magazine publisher, consultant and head of a training organization-my schedule is packed.

—Storm Cunningham

I just had my one year anniversary on PodMatch! Thanks for creating a great platform enabling me and others to have diverse conversations PodMatch is the BEST!!!

—Kevin McShan

PUBLISHED BY BITE SIZED BOOKS

Copyright © 2022 Bite Sized Books

Printed in the United States of America

Print ISBN: 978-1-7341187-6-6

101722

The publisher gratefully acknowledges the contributing authors who granted permission to reprint the cited material.

This publication is designed to provide accurate and helpful information with regard to the subject matter covered. It is sold with the understanding that the publisher is not engaged in rendering legal, accounting, or other professional advice. If legal advice or other expert assistance is required, the services of a competent professional should be sought. The opinions expressed by the authors in this book are not endorsed by Bite Sized Books and are the sole responsibility of the author rendering the opinion.

Bite Sized Books publishes short, helpful books for business owners, entrepreneurs and corporate leaders who are looking to stand out and differentiate their businesses. Do you have an idea for a bite sized book you would like us to publish? Visit BiteSizedBooks.com for more details.

CONTENTS

PART 3–BONUS RESOURCES

This book is dedicated to all the podcast hosts and guests
who are positively changing the world with their messages.

PART 1

WELCOME

ACKNOWLEDGEMENTS

First and foremost, I want to thank the members/ community of PodMatch for giving me the chance to help support them in finding podcasts to be a guest on. Thank you for trusting me to help you expand your influence!

I want to thank Jesus for giving me the courage to step out of my comfort zone and for the ability to execute this idea. My faith in Jesus is the foundation for the culture we've created within PodMatch!

What we're accomplishing with PodMatch wouldn't be possible without my tech-savvy cofounder, Jesse Hunter. Jesse, you're one of the most brilliant developers I've ever met, an excellent business partner, and the best friend a guy could ever hope to have. You have truly brought PodMatch to life!

I'd like to thank my favorite person, Alecia Sanfilippo. She's incredible when it comes to tackling challenging tasks and supporting members of the community. Without Alecia, I would have never gotten into podcasting in the first place. And without her belief in my ability to lead this business, I would still be in a corporate job. And without her devotion to showing up to serve the PodMatch community every day, you'd all have a lot of questions unanswered! Thank you, Alecia, for being my wife and partner in this journey!

I want to thank each of this book's contributing authors and Mike Capuzzi for putting PodMatch Guest Mastery together. Thank you so much for being PodMatch members and being willing to share your best tips and ideas for using PodMatch. I trust readers will learn much from your success, wisdom, and insights!

Lastly, I want to thank you, the reader. If you've picked up this book, that shows me that you will become a valuable member of the PodMatch community. Thank you for investing in yourself! I sincerely hope to get the opportunity to connect with you soon.

—Alex Sanfilippo

INTRODUCTION

"Hey Alex," Jesse asked, "Have we thought about how we're going to get people who want to be guests on podcasts to join PodMatch? I mean, I get that hosts are looking for guests, but do people really want to be guests on podcasts?"

This was a very insightful question. It hit me pretty hard because I realized I had validated the problem for hosts; they were having trouble finding guests. But I never considered the fact that maybe people don't actually want to be on podcasts as a guest.

This was an area of risk for PodMatch as we rapidly approached the June 15th, 2020, launch week.

We did an early beta with 100 podcast hosts a week before launching. Over the next few days, we had some guests start to trickle in, but not many.

I decided to reach out to a few friends who were public speakers. Because of the tough time the world was facing, I just wanted to encourage them and check in. I was conversing with a friend who was a traveling keynote speaker, and he said, "What are you up to during this time man? How are you?"

I explained PodMatch to him. He about jumped through the screen and said, "Are you serious??? MAN! This is the virtual stage I've been searching for."

I hadn't considered that before. Through other conversations with friends, I quickly realized that newly published authors (whether that be their first or next book) were also looking to do virtual book tours. I also discovered that coaches, entrepreneurs, and people with a message of hope/inspiration were all looking for the same thing—a platform to share their message. And podcasting had just become the most effective way to do that.

On June 15th, 2020, my wife (Alecia) and I posted a picture of us holding a laptop with the PodMatch logo on it. We explained that we designed it to help podcasters find guests and also help speakers, authors, coaches, entrepreneurs, and people with a message that would serve the world. We shared the tagline:

"A software that automatically matches ideal podcast guests and hosts for interviews."

That was my first (and only) "viral" social media post. Over the next week, we had thousands of people sign up to join PodMatch.

I am thankful to be years into this project now and serving tens of thousands of podcast guests and hosts. Beyond that, and ultimately, I'm even more grateful for the interview podcast episodes that have been released to serve the world of podcast listeners. Together, we're making the world a better place!

Because of PodMatch's exponential growth, we published this compilation book featuring some of the most successful PodMatch members worldwide. We believe this is the best way for current and future members of our growing community to learn from some individuals who have learned to maximize their experience with PodMatch.

As you read, you'll discover that PodMatch Guest Mastery includes different perspectives and insights on how to use PodMatch to get on other people's podcasts. This book aims to help you find your flow with PodMatch so you can also become a master of the platform!

Like podcast guesting, each contributing author has their own way of using PodMatch, and while there will be similarities between how members use the platform, there will also be distinct and valuable differences.

As a result of reading this book, I pray that you find the most ideal podcasts to be a guest on so that you can change lives with your content while continuing to grow your influence.

—Alex Sanfilippo

NOT A PODMATCH
MEMBER YET?

PodMatch is the premier site for entrepreneurs, thought leaders, and influencers to be automatically matched and find some of the world's top podcasts and be a featured guest.

With two value-packed membership levels, joining PodMatch is one of the smartest and most cost-effective ways to share your message on others' podcast shows.

Joining the PodMatch family is quick and simple. Just visit:

https://podmatch.com/signup/today

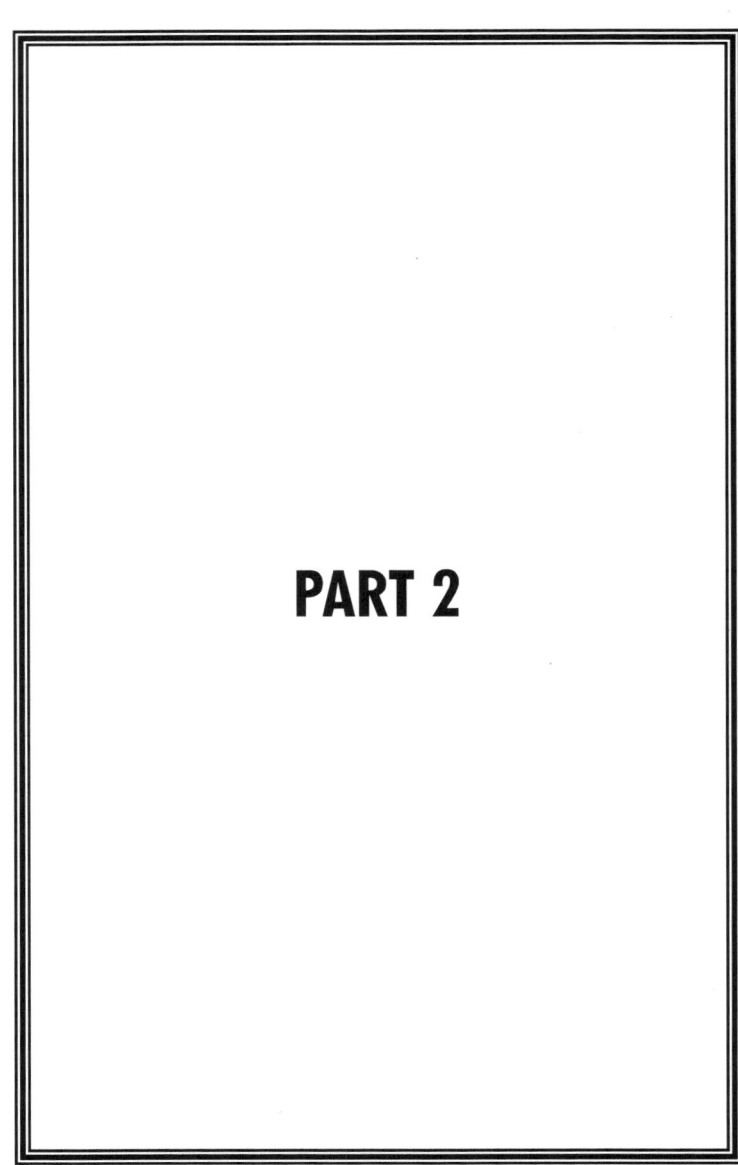

PART 2

THE PODCAST GUESTS

Mike Capuzzi

https://podmatch.com/member/mike-capuzzi

Mike is an author, a nonfiction book coach, and publisher of short books for business owners, entrepreneurs and CEOs looking to leverage the power of being an author of a short, helpful book.

Since 1998, Mike has helped thousands of business owners market their business smarter. Bite Sized Books, his book publishing company, was founded on his proven formula for creating short, helpful books (shooks™). Shooks are the ideal type of book to publish because they are easy and fast to create, can be read in about an hour and offer helpful ways for readers to connect with the author.

Mike is the author of 16 books, including two international Amazon # 1 Best Sellers. He is also the host of "The Author Factor Podcast" where he interviews business owner authors. Visit:

https://MikeCapuzzi.com

https://AuthorFactor.com

CHAPTER #1

MIKE CAPUZZI

Why did you join PodMatch as a Podcast Guest member?

I first learned about PodMatch in the summer of 2021. At that time, I had been hosting my own show and guesting on other shows for about 18 months. My guesting strategy was focused on finding and researching suitable shows and contacting the show's host and letting them know about the value I could offer their listeners.

This was time-intensive and tedious, so when I learned about PodMatch, I immediately signed up as a paid member. And to say I am a fan of Pod-Match is an understatement. I love what Alex and his team have built because it makes podcast guesting so much easier! The automated matching technology makes finding ideal shows for me fast and simple. To date, I have been a guest on more than 60 shows, and tens of thousands of listeners have heard my message.

What is one significant way that PodMatch has helped your business/mission?

Keeping this to just one thing is a challenge because so many cool things have happened as a result of being on PodMatch. I have met a bunch of supersmart and successful people I would have not met otherwise. Just this week, I signed a joint venture agreement with a show host I met on PodMatch that has the potential to generate a six-figure revenue stream for both of us. This deal would have never happened if I had not been a guest on his show.

What is your daily routine in PodMatch?

After studying one of the most successful Pod-Match Guests, Sean Tyler Foley (see Chapter #6), I changed how I used PodMatch. During my first months, I would log in sporadically, and since I did not have a specific strategy (wish I had this book back then), my initial results were "just OK."

Tyler encouraged me to be much more intentional and to log into PodMatch at least three times a day. As soon as I started to do this, my results improved. Since I am both a Podcast Guest and Host at the Professional level, I am in PodMatch at least three times a day. I actively go through the suggested matches and connect with hosts where I know I can add value and serve their listeners.

What do you recommend as the first thing a new Podcast Guest member should do after joining PodMatch?

Read this book ☺, but since you already are, definitely go through the PodMatch Education videos Alex created. Don't just have them playing in the background. Study and apply what he shares starting on day one.

What do you recommend as the second thing a new Podcast Guest member should do after joining PodMatch?

Create a powerful Guest Profile. Study the Guest Profiles of all the members in this book. (See their links in the Bonus Resources.) Create excellent content for all these parts, including:

- Your Video Pitch.
- Your tagline under your name.
- Your Guest Tags.
- Your Images.
- Your Biography.
- Your Desired CTA.
- Your "About You."
- Your "Learn About You" social media links.
- Suggested Episode Titles.
- Suggested Questions to ask you.

What "beginner's mistake" did you make with PodMatch that you want to warn other members about?

I briefly mentioned this earlier, but my biggest "newbie" mistake was that I didn't create and follow a specific and daily PodMatch Guest strategy. Yes, PodMatch is an automated matching system, but your part is not automated. This means that you or someone on your team must be actively going into PodMatch each day (at least 2x) and going through your suggested matches and exploring PodMatch Hosts. PodMatch only works effectively if you do your part every day to use it the way it was designed to be used.

The other mistake I made early on was that I expected every PodMatch Host to respond to my messages to be on their show. Here is the reality: There will be many hosts that you message that you will never hear from. Don't take it personally.

What three PodMatch best practices should every Podcast Guest use regularly?

1) Use it daily.

2) Create personalized and custom pitches to hosts. Do research and explain how you can add specific value to them and their show.

3) Tweak your Guest Tags to see if you get better matches.

What smart tip can you share for any Podcast Guest to use immediately and benefit from?

Most podcast hosts offer the opportunity to share how listeners can learn more about you at the conclusion of the interview. And this is where many guests make a BIG MISTAKE, when all they do is to share their website URL or social media profiles. While this is OK, it's what I call "plain vanilla" and doesn't make you stand out. The good news is that it can be easily improved for both the listener and you. Listen to any podcast episode I am guest on, and you will hear exactly how I use this two-step strategy.

Step 1: Before we start recording, I ask the host if it is OK to offer listeners a gift at the end. To date, 100% have enthusiastically said YES.

Step 2: When prompted by the host, instead of sharing my website or social media profiles, I let listeners know I have a valuable gift for them and direct them to a hidden page on my website. Nobody knows about this page, unless they heard about it on a podcast. You can see what my current one looks like on the next page.

This has a ton of value for listeners, but it also allows you to build your email database for future follow-up. An added benefit is that it allows me to know which podcast a listener heard me on.

Thank You for Listening to My Interview!

s I mentioned on the podcast, I have three short, helpful books (shooks) for you to read online for free! Simply enter our name, email and the name of the podcast you heard me on and I will send you an email with the shook links!

Screenshot of My Hidden "Listener Gift" Page

What smart tip can you share to help others get on podcasts where they and their message can have the most impact?

I am a fan of using a narrow guest strategy versus a wider strategy. For me, it is more important to be on a shorter list of shows where my ideal target prospect is listening (e.g., marketing and sales-related business podcasts) versus a longer list of shows that are not focused on the specific person I can help with my content.

So, my suggestion is to consider that **less can mean more!** Search and match with shows where you have a high level of confidence your ideal listener is listening and where your message or content will have the most impact. This narrower focus will allow you to create a more personal and relevant message to show hosts that specifically describes how you can help, transform, and/or motivate their listeners.

What is your final PodMatch "one thing" you want to leave readers with?

Alex and his team have built a Ferrari for matching podcast hosts with guests, automatically. But like any high-performance car, it requires high-quality fuel to run optimally. I believe PodMatch will help you achieve your podcasting goals if you put the right fuel into it.

What is that fuel?

It's your consistent, intentional, and smart use of it. This is the book I wish I had a year ago. Use it to enable you to share your message, impact lives and maximize your PodMatch membership!

Daniel Sih

https://podmatch.com/member/danielsih

Daniel is the co-founder of Spacemakers®, a productivity company for busy leaders. He is passionate about helping busy people make space in the digital age to do their best work and live their best life.

As a trainer, coach and keynote speaker, Daniel has worked with CEOs, executives, and other senior professionals throughout Australia and beyond.

He lives in Tasmania, Australia, with his wife, Kylie, and three children, Naomi, Caleb and Jethro. He also keeps 14 purebred chickens who eat a lot of grain and lay too few eggs.

To find out more about Daniel and his productivity courses, check out his websites:

https://Spacemakers.com.au

https://EmailNinja.com.au

CHAPTER #2

DANIEL SIH

Why did you join PodMatch as a Podcast Guest member?

It started with an idea: *"What if I could speak on 100 podcasts in the next 12 months? How much would that change my life?"*

As a first-time author, I was struggling to sell books internationally and get my message about "making space" into the world. Speaking on podcasts seemed to be a smart way to achieve my goals and grow my audience globally. *But how might I make this happen?*

As a productivity consultant, I understand the importance of breaking goals into actionable next steps, so I came up with a plan. I began contacting people in my professional networks and secured a handful of podcasts. This was time-consuming and unlikely to help me reach my goal. Next, I contacted podcasts outside of my networks without any success. Next, I considered hiring a marketing company, but costs were prohibitive. Thankfully, I stumbled upon a friend with podcasting experience, and they gave me some great advice: "*Just sign up to PodMatch!*"

Someone recently asked me to explain how I manage to line up so many podcasts so quickly. My secret? "*Just sign up to PodMatch!*"

What is one significant way that PodMatch has helped your business/mission?

PodMatch has helped me to grow professionally and share my mission with a global audience in three ways:

1) It expanded my professional networks, connecting me with amazing people from around the world.

2) It allowed me to improve my communication skills through hundreds of long-form conversations. These interviews have made me a better podcast guest and helped me to clarify my vision and tighten my message.

3) It helped me to overcome "imposter syndrome," building my confidence in answering questions in front of a global audience. This has helped me to project myself positively in other forums as a productivity knowledge expert.

What is your daily routine in PodMatch?

This changes depending on whether I have space in my schedule for more interviews.

If I am looking to secure more interviews, I log on to PodMatch each day and write between four to ten messages to reach out to potential hosts.

If my guest interview schedule is already at capacity, I only check PodMatch every few days to respond to new messages.

What do you recommend as the first thing a new Podcast Guest member should do after joining PodMatch?

Create a clear and compelling profile, completing all the sections in the profile template. The clearer you are about your core message, the more likely you will be to attract relevant podcast hosts.

What do you recommend as the second thing a new Podcast Guest member should do after joining PodMatch?

Get active in writing personalized messages to potential hosts, rather than using a generic template. When I started using PodMatch, I sent 50 unique messages over a few weeks, keeping my eye out for words or phrases that resulted in positive responses. Eventually, I created a Word document with templates for various subjects, such as productivity podcasts, parenting podcasts, or health podcasts, to speed up future communications. Even still, these templates are only a starting point. I continue to customize each message where possible.

What "beginner's mistake" did you make with PodMatch that you want to warn other members about?

When people ask me to explain how PodMatch works, I cheekily say, "*It's like Tinder for podcasters*." You create a profile. You hook up with potential hosts. You click "pass" or "match" based on whether you like each other.

I'm a married man with three children and have never used a dating app, so PodMatch is as close as I get to booking dates with strangers! When I first joined the community, it was a rush to have people accept my messages with a "match." Before long, I had a string of ~~hot dates~~ interviews with intelligent, creative podcasters from around the world.

Energized, I started checking my account three or four times a day, spending hours communicating with various hosts. My ego expanded when my name began to appear on the PodMatch leaderboard—the list of most eligible podcast bachelors—especially when I reached the top spot for a day. Here's the problem. In my excitement, I started to lose sight of the main game. Rather than aiming for quality, I focused on quantity and ran out of time for other things.

This was my beginner's mistake—getting excited and booking so many interviews that I ran out of space for paid clients, administration, and other time needed for family life. Not smart.

After a few weeks, I realised that staying on the leaderboard was counter to my message of "making space for what matters most." Podcasting is a means to an end—sharing a message with the world and driving meaningful business—not the goal itself. Now I commit to one or two podcasts a week, at sensible times in the day, rather than boom and bust with an overcommitment of five to eight interviews a week.

What three PodMatch best practices should every Podcast Guest use regularly?

1) Listen to every podcast before you begin an interview to ensure you understand the tone, energy levels and general vibe of the program in advance.

2) Prepare well, but be flexible in what you talk about, ensuring that you answer questions that the host asks you rather than sticking to a formulaic script.

3) Be willing to be vulnerable and authentic in the interview, sharing something of yourself and your own struggles. People want to hear from a human being, not just an expert with wins and successes.

What smart tip can you share for any Podcast Guest to use immediately and benefit from?

Set up for quality sound recording. This is important for podcast hosts. Having previously recorded an audiobook, I had a high-quality microphone, fast Internet, and a quiet home office with sound-dampening panels. This setup was worth the investment.

What smart tip can you share to help others get on podcasts where they and their message can have the most impact?

Be selective in who you reach out to and why you are messaging them. Podcast hosts are looking for guests who genuinely align with their shows. Before the interview, I ask every host to describe their audience—entrepreneurs, C-suite executives, busy parents, health professionals—and what they hope to gain from the interview. By truly understanding their audience, I am more able to craft my language and stories to address their specific needs. Every interview should be different and address specific people.

Ultimately, the aim is to serve the host's audience rather than yourself. The more you can do this, the better the interview will be. By providing great content, you will get more interviews. It's as simple and as difficult as this.

What is your final PodMatch "one thing" you want to leave readers with?

There is intrinsic value to being a podcast guest, beyond any tangible benefits received. For myself, speaking to a global audience is an expression of who I am as a person. I get to help thousands of people with a message that changes lives. I get to meet interesting people. I get to learn and grow personally.

In my thinking, you will succeed as a PodMatch Podcast Guest if you find intrinsic value in the process. Embrace podcasting as a way of serving the community, not just achieving your commercial goals. This doesn't mean that there aren't financial benefits of putting yourself "out there." The marketing value and brand exposure can be tremendously valuable. But own your message internally, not just externally. Be motivated to improve other people's lives and you will be successful as a podcast guest.

Best of luck!

Andrea Petrut

Andrea Petrut is a fierce advocate for love and healing, and this thread weaves through everything she does as an engaging visionary speaker, teacher, workshop leader, trauma-informed facilitator, home educator, storyteller, somatic writer (currently writing a hybrid memoir), host of "Healing Through Oneness" podcast, and podcast guest.

She is passionate about co-empowering women globally to embrace their uniqueness and courageously lead the change. Her warm presence encourages inspired thoughts and deeper insight that allows individuals to reach into themselves and find answers there.

https://AndreaPetrut.ca

CHAPTER 3

ANDREA PETRUT

Why did you join PodMatch as a Podcast Guest member?

In the fall of 2021, I started my own series of interviews live on social media, but I didn't know I was "podcasting" and wasn't thinking of being a guest myself. I just wanted to give a shout out to changemakers I believed in. Then I found from a mastermind friend, Roy Coughlan (from the "Speaking Podcast"), that his interview with Sean Tyler Foley could help me in my speaking career. When my friends and mentors guide me to a name, I dive in. That's how I stumbled upon a 2016 video about his BHAG (big hairy goal) of reaching 10M people. I didn't dare have the same goal, so I picked 20x less (very big still for me).

I started following him and Michael Harris, learning and applying. I did my own research and found other platforms but none were as organized, easy to use, transparent and fruitful in the sense I understood what was possible. Inspired and supported, I became fascinated with the immense potential of podcasting nowadays for me. Making impact and sharing my message of healing, deep transformation and oneness in the world is my priority. I remembered my BHAG and became a paid member because I wanted to use the platform fully. I became eager to be among leaders and catalysts for big impact and global change. And I had both these guys to show me the exact steps to make it happen through speaking on podcasts.

What is one significant way that PodMatch has helped your business/mission?

The list keeps growing, and it's hard to pick just one. But what I care about the most that helps me with my work in the world are the friendships and collaborations with people I wouldn't have met in my everyday life. Extraordinary leaders and hosts have become mentors, co-teachers, and great supporters. We're helping each other's goals and build projects that otherwise wouldn't have been possible if we didn't meet for their podcasts. It's mind-blowing how I resonated in very deep ways with others just by exchanging messages or simply by them looking at my profile photo.

What is your daily routine in PodMatch?

I went full on and applied everything very fast, blocking space in my schedule. The best is when I check matches two to three times a day. Out of the matches, I pin the best ones I want to connect with in the moment and set time aside for deeper research. If I'm hooked after looking through some details, I then check the show description, stats, and their ideal type of guest. I check if the podcast is still running and then read about the show and host. I always get a feel of the podcast and host by listening to one or two episodes. To be sure we're a match and to make a good proposal, I look at titles, people they interview, and topics to discover what I can bring of value. When I understand where my approach could be of service to the host and their audience, I message the host, tapping into all those observations.

What do you recommend as the first thing a new Podcast Guest member should do after joining PodMatch?

Get used to the platform and all the pieces of it. The dashboard is the most exciting thing to start with. Only by exploring that will you get the best of it, especially the tutorials. Alex made sure his videos are clear and the learning curve for you is short. Be smart and apply right away. *Action is alchemy!*

What do you recommend as the second thing a new Podcast Guest member should do after joining PodMatch?

Make sure your Guest Profile is compelling and really mirroring who you are and how you serve in the world. Follow the best practices for each section. You save yourself time, tears and start on the right foot by looking at the top guests. This book is the best resource plus the current live top 10. Notice commonalities and differences of the profiles of at least three of them or from your favorites. Model what best suits your goals, message and personality. Implement and update the more you get used to what works and what doesn't work for you.

What "beginner's mistake" did you make with PodMatch that you want to warn other members about?

I did quite a few, but the most significant was going through the matches and not writing hosts the same day I found a resonance. I missed opportunities. I filled my list of pinned podcasts and then didn't have more room to add to it. Plus, it took me longer to review and message them if I left too much time to pass because I forgot why I picked them in the first place, even if I left a note with keywords for each.

What three PodMatch best practices should every Podcast Guest use regularly?

1) Check your matches and messages often. Don't rely on the platform to remind you or notify you. Make your own notes. Communications with hosts may be surprising, and it's not always possible to track everything automatically. If the host has seen your message but hasn't answered, let it be. If they wrote back proposing for you to be on the wait list and you said yes, then set a reminder for a follow-up with them at a later date.

2) The system found a match. First check if the podcast is still running. Some hosts appear on PodMatch, but they paused their show or don't have the engagement you're looking for.

3) Be open-minded with the PodMatch rating for a host. It may not reflect the quality of the interviewer or the show at all. Focus on your mission and your priorities while looking at the stats. Listen to the show, and make your own opinion. Maybe the host is the type of rebel not everyone likes, but you do. Maybe the host uses language some don't find appropriate, but it's your lan-

guage. and you don't care what others think and you want in.

What smart tip can you share for any Podcast Guest to use immediately and benefit from?

Use the platform like your own home: Knock on the doors of people you would feel inspired by and supported by and allow into your life, e.g., hosts who want to be of service and contribute to your mission while bringing value to their own creations. Keep it tidy; don't let relationships linger in the air. Either you want to be on a show or you don't. If you don't feel ready, pin them for a later check-in with yourself. Pick the best ones you feel pulled to, and let the others sit lower in your list of preferences. Always engage right away with hosts that message you because it will spark attention. And be mindful; they don't have much time. For most of them, it's a hobby in a busy schedule. Respect that.

What smart tip can you share to help others get on podcasts where they and their message can have the most impact?

Find congruency, the best fit between your message, the host (podcast) and the audience.

What is your final PodMatch "one thing" you want to leave readers with?

PodMatch is still an unused resource by many who have stories and messages the world needs to hear. It is an oyster for those looking for self-growth and reaching their greatness, launching into the world and expanding personally and professionally alongside and thanks to like-minded and like-hearted people.

I invite you to see this platform as your training camp or an adventure of a lifetime. It's a curated, carefully organized, and heartfelt community to bring out the beautiful, gifted human that you are and we all need now in these times. Stretch your comfort zone, and make sure what your heart/gut is telling you is what you follow. Amazing opportunities for business, collaboration or your own life come in unexpected ways.

Tonya Eberhart & Michael Carr

https://podmatch.com/member/brandfacestar

Tonya and Michael are international bestselling authors, coaches, speakers, hosts of the "Be BOLD Branding" podcast, and partners in BrandFace™, the most comprehensive personal brand-building system across the globe.

Their passion is unveiling inner stars.

Their mantra is "People don't do business with a logo. They do business with a person."

Their most famous quote is "Great branding doesn't just change the way others see you. It changes the way you see yourself."

They have helped and inspired podcasters, authors, coaches, sales professionals, and business owners in 5 countries and 45 U.S. states to become an authority, out-market, and outsell their competitors through the power of personal branding.

http://BrandFaceStar.com

TONYA EBERHART & MICHAEL CARR

Why did you join PodMatch as a Podcast Guest member?

There are now almost three million podcasts, but the number of potential guests is far greater. We were seeking a platform in which we could position ourselves as personal branding authorities with a unique message. PodMatch allowed us to showcase our own brand, thus attracting hosts who needed our expertise. It has given us the opportunity to match with hosts in just one click, and manage those connections under one roof, from introduction to interview. As a result, we have not only gained publicity and credibility as expert guests, but we have also built relationships as affiliates, clients, and partners through PodMatch introductions.

What is one significant way that PodMatch has helped your business/mission?

We have been booked as expert guests on more than 70 podcasts (in the last 7 months), designed to position us as authorities in the world of personal branding. This value alone is immeasurable because someone else (the host) is advocating for us and our business just by interviewing us for their show. Because of these appearances and the hosts who have so graciously invited us to be on their shows, we have attracted clients, affiliates, partners, and friends from all over the world. Today, podcast appearances bring us qualified prospects and closed deals, resulting in a main source of revenue for our company.

What is your daily routine in PodMatch?

The first thing we do each day is to check the "matches" section inside the PodMatch dashboard. We research the hosts who have reached out to us and make sure that our target criteria match. After that, we check our "messages" section to respond or communicate regarding the booking process. Finally, we head to the "explore" section and choose keywords on the search bar that are aligned to our topics in order to find new possible podcasts with the same target audience. Once we've finished searching, we check our to-do list and mark the items that have been completed. By following these simple steps, we've matched successfully to an average of ten hosts per month.

What do you recommend as the first thing a new Podcast Guest member should do after joining PodMatch?

Before you spend one dollar or one more day promoting yourself as a potential guest, make sure you build the brand that supports your authority. You need to be clear about what makes you different, who you help, how you help them, and what qualifies you to help them in order for you to build a profile attractive enough for prospective hosts. Your personal brand will help you differentiate yourself from the other guests (especially in the same space) and unveil the unique value that you bring to the table. Without these steps, it will be difficult for you to rise to the top of the guest leaderboard. Remember that there are literally thousands of potential guests for each show topic, and your goal is to stand out as the guest who brings a unique spin and incredible value.

What do you recommend as the second thing a new Podcast Guest member should do after joining PodMatch?

Once your brand is well defined, then consistency becomes the key factor in your success. First, be consistent when it comes to your value, and be consistent in how you show up. When a podcast host values your time enough to feature you in an episode, value his/her time by being punctual, prepared, and respectful. Take the time to dress appropriately (just in case the host utilizes video in addition to audio), and make sure your background reflects your brand, as well. Remember, your appearance is as much about you and what you stand for as it is about your host and their show. Finally, be consistent in your follow-up after an interview. Leave your host a positive review, and send a thank you card or a simple gift for their time and thoughtfulness. Those small things go a long way to bring positivity to everyone involved in the podcast world.

What "beginner's mistake" did you make with PodMatch that you want to warn other members about?

First, don't send the same message to every host you're pitching. Take the time to read the host's profile and guest criteria and visit their website and social channels. And definitely listen to two or three of their podcast episodes. These simple steps will help you land more appearances because you can speak to specific and personalized topics when you pitch the host. Those same steps are even more important once you land the appearance because unless you know how the host conducts themselves and what they're seeking from their guests, you will likely be unprepared. Remember that your goal as a guest is to provide unparalleled content and be so valuable that you get invited back again to finish the conversation!

What three PodMatch best practices should every Podcast Guest use regularly?

1) Do your homework on your hosts and be a prepared guest.

2) Reply to all of your messages in a timely manner and with kindness.

3) Give back to your hosts. (A review, thank you card, a simple gift, or a referral are the best options.)

What smart tip can you share for any Podcast Guest to use immediately and benefit from?

If you're not sure how to define or choose your ideal customer, use our exclusive H.E.A.P. Code™ to narrow your approach, and ensure that you are speaking to and attracting exactly who you want in your business and your life. H.E.A.P. is an acronym, and here's the breakdown:

H stands for HELP: Identify someone you can truly help. Perhaps you can help this person because you have been through a similar circumstance or phase of life, you have expertise in a specific area, or you simply connect well with that type of person.

E stands for ENJOY: Identify someone you enjoy working with because life is too short to dance with ugly personalities. If we don't enjoy what we do and the people we do it for, what is the point?

A stands for APPRECIATE: Identify someone who truly appreciates your value and will let you do your job. We've all worked with someone who second-guesses our every move or thinks they know better. And we know exactly how it feels when they appreciate us.

P stands for PROFIT: Identify someone who is profitable for you. Profit is a positive word. We are all in business to make a profit. Keep in mind that this doesn't necessarily mean that this client buys your most expensive product or service. It could be that, of course, but it could also be someone who buys from you more consistently or refers you to more people just like them.

What smart tip can you share to help others get on podcasts where they and their message can have the most impact?

Create two or three different templates of the message you'll send to each host with sections that allow you to adapt the message to what they are looking for and test which one has the best results. This will help you increase your closing rates and hone in on your own message at the same time.

What is your final PodMatch "one thing" you want to leave readers with?

Do not promote yourself before having a clear and strong personal brand that showcases your value through a unique message and congruent image. Your chances of being selected as a guest are incredibly higher when you know how to clearly express why people should choose you and what sets you apart from everyone else in your space. You have just one chance for that first impression, so make sure you nail it!

Chris Williams

Chris spends most of his time raising his five kids, exploring world communities, and trying his hand at adventures like shark diving, ice climbing, running ultramarathons, and riding electric skateboards.

In his spare time, he works with entrepreneurial and business experts, speakers, coaches, and leaders helping them market, monetize, and lead their own high-ticket mastermind (or group coaching) programs. As the world continues to shift, many experts are trying to build high-ticket groups for additional income, lead generation, or impact. Chris teaches experts how to generate leads, close high-ticket deals, and build strong, transformational groups. He has his own digital agency, leads two masterminds of his own, and has learned many of these lessons the hard way, so sharing his journey and offering strategies is why he is here.

https://GroupCoachNation.com

CHAPTER #5

CHRIS WILLIAMS

Why did you join PodMatch as a Podcast Guest member?

Aren't you loving this book so far? They only gave me 1,500 words (I guess I talk too much!), so I will be as concise as possible so I can show you how to make money as a guest on PodMatch today! I joined because PodMatch is THE easiest way to find podcast hosts who can become my clients. You don't even need to have your own podcast to use PodMatch to make money!

What is one significant way that PodMatch has helped your business/mission?

PodMatch makes it very easy for me to meet the right people with the right audiences, and there-fore, generates high-quality leads for me to sell to. I teach experts how to build high-ticket master-minds, so podcast hosts are a natural market for my service. Podcast guesting has helped my business grow more than podcast hosting. My team reaches out to hosts who are my ideal clients, then the host reviews my profile and decides whether or not they are interested in what I have to say. This is so important because you're allowing the host to select you. If a host I've pre-screened asks me to be a guest, I know that they are not only my ideal client but also that they want what I have, so before I even show up to the interview, we are already halfway to the sale.

What is your daily routine in PodMatch?

A team member helps me search for the ideal host and audience combination where both the host and the audience could be clients. We reach out individually and let the host know we are fans and would be happy to support them and their audience in any way. If they think it's a good fit, they will offer to have me as a guest on their show. As a guest, I am doing a sort of "live discovery call" with the host, starting that relationship and helping with real advice wherever I can. If after the interview I think the relationship needs more work before the sell, I will either offer to have them as a guest on my show or I'll offer a free strategy call as a way to return the favor. They almost always take me up on this offer. This has worked so well for me that I actually teach this process in my mastermind, explaining exactly how to monetize PodMatch and podcasting as a guest. Sadly, I can't expound more here because I've been given a strict word count limit and am already at word 440! I am, however, including a full checklist of exactly how we do this along with a flowchart illustrating my process as a free gift.

What do you recommend as the first thing a new Podcast Guest member should do after joining PodMatch?

Build your PodMatch profile completely and strategically. A member of our mastermind, Phil Pelucha, is a great example of this. His PodMatch profile, along with his other social profiles, displays his expertise in an attractive way to his ideal audience. Nothing new there, right? However, most podcasters build their profile with the podcast audience in mind. The trick is building your profile with the podcast host in mind. Your profile should be crafted to make you an attractive guest to the hosts you ultimately want to sell to. Fill in all the fields of your profile completely to help the host. Your bio section should be written to intrigue the host. By looking at your profile, the host should know that you'd be easy to interview and that you have interesting things to say that they would benefit from hearing. Feel free to check out my profile as an example!

What do you recommend as the second thing a new Podcast Guest member should do after joining PodMatch?

Optimize your searching parameters so you find hosts and audiences who are ideal clients. Again, get the PodMatch Pro membership! It's so worth it because it gives you a better search process you don't get with the free version, and it shows hosts you're the real deal since your profile will show that you've invested in Pro. Search using keywords to get to your target market (author, marketing, branding, etc.). You can narrow it down by ratings or whatever you want, but find the right search parameters to find your target audience. Then find a host, do research on them, and reach out if they're a fit. You can delegate this process easily; that's what I do!

What "beginner's mistake" did you make with PodMatch that you want to warn other members about?

I didn't know you could leave and receive reviews on PodMatch for an embarrassingly long time! Now, I love leaving reviews for other amazing hosts. Reviews build out profiles and relational capital with the hosts who, remember, you're ultimately trying to sell to.

What three PodMatch best practices should every Podcast Guest use regularly?

1) Be picky in choosing the right hosts and audiences. Your time is valuable, and so is the host's. You don't want to waste time on a show whose host and audience aren't genuinely interested in what you have to say.

2) Be consistent in your usage of PodMatch! Find the right balance with your schedule, and send the right amount of outreach messages weekly to fill the time you have set aside to be interviewed. For example, maybe the right balance is finding one host in your target market a day and starting a conversation. Whatever your balance is, strike the right one and stick to it. Again, this is so easy to delegate!

3) Show up for every podcast like it's the biggest stage in the world. Half-assing doesn't help you, the host, or the audience. Bring your A game, and remember to treat it like an extended sales call (without being pushy or weird). Another one of my mastermind members, Kim Garst, is the ultimate example of this! She gives 100% as both the keynote speaker at a huge in-person event and the interview on the smallest podcast like the pro she is.

What smart tip can you share for any Podcast Guest to use immediately and benefit from?

Be a giver. Jhana Li, who is in our Group Coach Nation Pro Mastermind, is a rockstar at showing up to give, and it has delivered her many dividends! If you're the host or the audience listening to Jhana speak, you walk away with real, actionable things to do. Make sure your host WINS.

What smart tip can you share to help others get on podcasts where they and their message can have the most impact?

Only talk to hosts who are your ideal client! Think about it this way: If you're in the business of sharing your expertise, then the best thing you can do for the host and the listeners is confirm they are the right people before you ever start talking. Ideal prospects will love what you say more than anyone else. You're trying to sell, but you're also genuinely offering what your ideal prospect wants. It's a win-win.

Here's my smart tip: Once you've guested on a show, browse other episodes to find who else has guested on that show; they are likely in your target market as well. You can also research what shows the host has been a guest on to find more quality leads. When you message these leads on PodMatch, use the fact that you've been on the same show or were on the show of one of their former guests as a connection point. It seriously works, so much so that I teach this process in my masterminds!

What is your final PodMatch "one thing" you want to leave readers with?

If you ever get a chance to be in a room with Alex Sanfilippo and the people he surrounds himself with—do it. He is the real deal and can help you get where you want to go. If it wasn't for his vision and generosity, you wouldn't be reading this chapter right now.

Finally, with monetizing guesting on podcasts and as with anything, my personal motto remains true: Do work; get results.

Aaagh, I'm at word 1,407! Okay, I've included a PDF checklist where I've laid out all the steps I've discussed on how to monetize guesting through PodMatch as a free gift (get it in the Bonus Resources section). This is the exact checklist we share with people in my mastermind, and in my experience teaching this, people usually have more questions. Reach out to us through our website or social media and my team will be happy to point you in the right direction!

Tyler Foley

Sean Tyler Foley is an accomplished film and stage performer and has been acting in film and television since he was six years old.

He has appeared in productions, including *Freddy vs. Jason, Door to Door, Carrie,* and the musical *Ragtime.* Tyler is passionate about helping others confidently take the stage and impact an audience with their stories. He is currently the managing director of TOTAL BUY IN and author of the #1 best-selling book, *The Power to Speak Naked.*

https://SeanTylerFoley.com

CHAPTER 6

TYLER FOLEY

Why did you join PodMatch as a Podcast Guest member?

I initially joined PodMatch as a guest member to promote my book, *The Power to Speak Naked*. I had been a professional speaker for years and knew that speaking opportunities were one of the best ways to promote my book and speaker training business. I also loved the idea of being able to meet fellow podcasters and build relationships in the industry.

What is one significant way that PodMatch has helped your business/mission?

PodMatch helped my business in multiple ways, but one of the most significant is in my search engine optimization. Over the last year, organically and without any input from me really, my SEO has skyrocketed because of the sheer volume of links and backlinks on major sites to my website. PodMatch has helped me to level up my speaking business by expanding my reach, building my authority, and creating new content opportunities. I've been a guest on over 300 podcasts, and many of those are syndicated on multiple channels. So, not only has PodMatch helped me get in front of more diverse audiences, it has also helped me get in front of more people in a way that search engines view as credible and trustworthy.

What is your daily routine in PodMatch?

Typically, I am checking PodMatch for matches three to four times a day. I am regularly messaging hosts and pitching episodes, approving matches, leaving reviews, and reviewing/updating my profile to make sure that my tags are relevant. I am also regularly checking and contributing to the PodPros.com community forums by answering questions and engaging with other members.

What do you recommend as the first thing a new Podcast Guest member should do after joining PodMatch?

The first thing I would recommend any new guest should do after joining PodMatch is to review and study the 10 training modules! They are quick and answer most of the frequently asked questions. PLUS, completing the training improves your ranking as a PodMatch guest.

What do you recommend as the second thing a new Podcast Guest member should do after joining PodMatch?

Get very clear about why you want to be a guest on podcasts and what your specific call-to-action will be. You want to be very clear about how you help your ideal client or what problem you solve for them. This will make it much easier to match with the right podcasts and also make a great impression when you do get booked as a guest. Be sure that your PodMatch profile reflects this by having a great picture, biography, and the correct tags.

I would also recommend that you start by creating a list of 10–15 podcasts that you would LOVE to be a guest on and then systematically begin pitching those shows.

What "beginner's mistake" did you make with PodMatch that you want to warn other members about?

Letting my matches sit without checking them. It is very important to clear through your matches regularly to take the most advantage of the system. Clearing through all the matches and allowing the system to reset and find new matches is when the true power of the platform is unlocked.

What three PodMatch best practices should every Podcast Guest use regularly?

1) Be diligent with responding back to messages quickly. This has multiple benefits. It shows that you are a reliable guest, helps the PodMatch system to know that you are active, and helps improve your overall ranking as a guest.

2) When pitching a show, remember that the pitch is not about you, it is about the show's audience and what you can provide them and do for them. Bring value to the table, and be clear about what that value is in your pitch, and you will find more hosts will want you on their shows.

3) As you start to do more shows, pay attention to the questions that organically come up regularly, and what your responses are, and then review and amend your "questions you are always ready to answer" section of your profile to reflect this. This will help both you and future hosts in creating a smooth and enjoyable interview for all parties— you, the host, and most importantly, the listeners.

What smart tip can you share for any Podcast Guest to use immediately and benefit from?

New matches may be available sooner than the stated prompt that is generated by PodMatch, sometimes as much as 30 minutes before. Checking early and often can sometimes get an extra "match cycle" in a day, which can have a very positive impact on your guest ranking.

Also, when completing your Guest Tags, if Pod-Match doesn't auto-complete the tag for you, then no one is looking for that tag. Remember, the Guest Tags are what PodMatch uses to connect hosts and guests. So if you are using a Guest Tag that PodMatch doesn't recognize, you are likely not going to come up in any search results, or the shows you do get matched with will not be as ideal as they could be. The biggest mistake I see new users make is by trying to use branded stages unique to them, which completely negates the search function. Use the About Me section of the profile to get in branding, not Guest Tags.

What smart tip can you share to help others get on podcasts where they and their message can have the most impact?

Make sure to tailor each pitch to the show and host. Even if you are using a templated pitch, which I do, customizing each message in some way is critical. No one wants a generic pitch, and they become pretty obvious. My best advice for PodMatch members who want to be selected as guests more often is to make sure that you have a strong profile and that you are regularly appearing in the search results of the hosts you want to match with. Spend a good amount of time crafting a compelling profile so that when a host is looking into you or is matched with you, they know EXACTLY who you are and what they are getting by having you on your show. Completing a video introduction is very helpful with this.

What is your final PodMatch "one thing" you want to leave readers with?

You have a story and a message that needs to be heard, and podcasting is one of the most efficient ways to get that out quickly and to a broad and diverse audience. PodMatch is hands down the best platform currently available to find those opportunities, not just as a technical service. Having used multiple matching platforms as a guest, I can confidently say that PodMatch is easily the best on the market, but what really makes it stand out is the community that has been built around the platform. Take advantage of that community to help spread your message and there are no limits to the impact that you could have.

PodMatch has given me the opportunity to speak on a variety of topics, not just promoting my book. I have also been able to connect with some amazing people and learn about new things. My favorite thing about PodMatch is the community. I have met so many amazing people from all over the world who are passionate about podcasting. PodMatch has also given me the opportunity to learn new things and grow as a speaker and author.

If you want to be a PodMatch success story, it really comes down to one thing: Take massive action and use the platform every day. The more you use PodMatch and the more active you are, the more likely you are to get booked on great podcasts, which will help grow your business. This is the formula I have used to become the top ranked guest on PodMatch over the last 18 months, and it is a formula that has worked for many other PodMatch members as well.

Michael Harris

https://podmatch.com/member/michaelharris

Michael is a lifelong entrepreneur, dynamic business coach, #1 bestselling author, remarkable storyteller, yoga teacher and co-founder of Endless Stages—a company dedicated to helping entrepreneurs, experts and authors get their voice, message and story out to the world with a bit of pizzazz on podcasts and stage.

His official goals include hiking and rambling up as many buttes as possible, without stumbling down. His even bigger goal is to jump across a deep, wide creek on a pogo stick or simply sip lemonade while watching someone else attempt it first. Regardless, whatever happens, he's bound to tell great adventurous stories about his latest business and personal escapades.

http://MichaelBHarris.com

http://EndlessStages.com

CHAPTER 7

MICHAEL HARRIS

Why did you join PodMatch as a Podcast Guest member?

At one point many years ago, I studied the art of storytelling at Marylhurst University. Really anything that had to do with telling stories, I was in. All stories, whether ancient myths, overcoming adversity, marketing and life in general, I wanted to hear and tell.

After publishing my first book, I hosted two of my own popular podcasts, reaching about 1,000 downloads a day. Starting with show-and-tell as a kid, I've always enjoyed telling stories.

Then, one of my business partners, Sean "Tyler" Foley, had previously joined PodMatch and was frequently at the top of the leaderboard as the #1 guest. One day, with a bit of fun, I told Tyler to watch out because I was going to knock him off the top. PodMatch was ringing out to me loud and clear.

Within about 45 days of enrolling, I hit the Pod-Match Guest Leaderboard—then quickly made it to the #1 spot—and continue to remain mostly in the top ten.

Today, I get to take my storytelling experience to help others get their own unique message and story to the world on podcasts, stages and business.

What is one significant way that PodMatch has helped your business/mission?

You never know who is listening. With that said, perhaps the most significant way that PodMatch has helped my mission and business are the connections I have made with others. Several partnerships and joint ventures have happened, including book proposals, virtual events and high-end trainings. I've actually had to turn down a few opportunities, simply because of a lack of time.

In addition, as someone that has been a teacher, coach and trainer for 30+ years, I've expanded my reach, authority and credibility to help others get their voice out on podcasts and stage.

What is your daily routine in PodMatch?

One of the first things I do every morning is to check what's happening on PodMatch. I review my suggested matches and check each one. I'll look at my messages and respond as soon as I can. When I find potential matches, I'll always take a look at their website and social media. Then I'll randomly listen to a few snippets of their episodes. This will help me know if we're a good match and give me ideas on how to reach out to them to be on their show.

Most days, I check my messages every four to six hours and go through the whole process again. I don't want to miss the possibility of any great podcasts and connections.

What do you recommend as the first thing a new Podcast Guest member should do after joining PodMatch?

Go through as much of the PodMatch platform as possible. Regardless, if you're new to podcasting or you have years of experience, study the available educational materials and videos to become a great guest. And click on the various top ten guests on the leaderboard.

What makes them stand out?

What does their profile look like?

What is their CTA?

See what's making them stand out and model (don't copy) what they are doing to get to the top.

What do you recommend as the second thing a new Podcast Guest member should do after joining PodMatch?

Consider the following:

Are you clear on your intentions of becoming a guest?

Do you know the messages and stories you want to tell?

Is your profile clear and defined so a host will want you on their show?

Have you created episode topics and questions that give you the results you want?

What benefit does podcasting guesting give to your business?

Does podcasting help spread a message to the audience you want?

What "beginner's mistake" did you make with PodMatch that you want to warn other members about?

Not checking my matches enough.

Be sure to check your matches and your messages several times a day. If you don't, you might miss out on shows and opportunities that fit perfectly into your message and your business.

What three PodMatch best practices should every Podcast Guest use regularly?

1) Check and review all matches several times a day. This will ensure you will continue to get matches, get booked and appear on the shows you want.

2) Reach out to at least one host a day. By contacting one host and one show a day, you'll start to get shows and be able to hone your pitches.

3) Review and adjust your profile. Oftentimes, the host will ask you different questions and have different episode ideas for a show with you. You might even see a pattern with this. Be willing to tweak your profile according to the shows you are getting and the feedback you are receiving.

What smart tip can you share for any Podcast Guest to use immediately and benefit from?

Regardless of the reason you joined PodMatch, you have a message and story that you want to get out to the world.

Your profile is essentially a hook, story and offer to get on a show and get you heard. *What is one thing you can do to "hook" a host to be on their show on their platform? What is the story and offer you are making to back up your hook?*

Knowing this is vital in attracting OPAs (other people's audiences) to build and grow your mission and business.

What smart tip can you share to help others get on podcasts where they and their message can have the most impact?

Take time to define and get clear on the message and story you want to talk about as a guest. Being clear on the story and message you want to tell will help you get on the shows that are most likely in alignment with your mission and business.

Consider the following:

1) *What is the result you want from being on podcasts?* A few options could include: building and growing your mailing list, people buying your services and/or your books.

2) *Who do you want to listen, and what action do you want them to take after listening to you?* Understand who your ideal avatar and customer is and what motivates them.

3) *What stories and messages can you use to get the result you want?* Find the stories about your business and life that resonate with your listener and get your listener to take action.

What is your final PodMatch "one thing" you want to leave readers with?

Do what you say you're going to do.

In other words, quickly follow up with messages from hosts. Complete the requested information. Be on time for recordings. Give the hosts reviews, and post the shows on your platform.

Make a commitment to not just be a good guest, but instead, be a great guest that goes the extra mile and gets invited back over and over again.

When that's done, your results will accelerate, and you'll be able to get the outcome you want to get your message and story to the world.

One more thing, **smile, have fun** and don't forget to download your free copy of *The Ultimate Guide to Being an Outrageously Great Podcast Guest* (see Bonus Resources section).

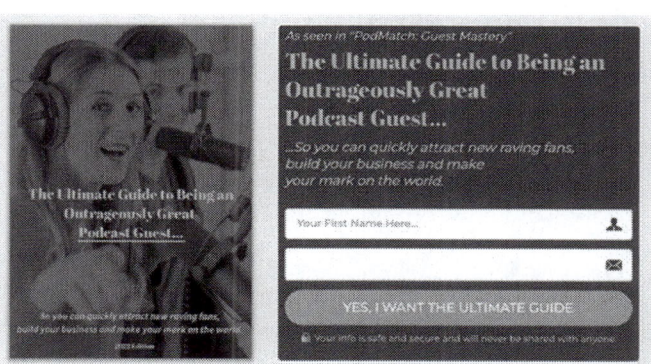

Wade Galt

Wade teaches entrepreneurs to create an abundant & sustainable 3-Day Weekend lifestyle so they can better enjoy their family, friends, and life. His coaching programs help entrepreneurs impact more people and make more money, in less time, doing what they do best.

It took him 7 years after graduating college to start his own business and 15 more years to create an abundant and sustainable 3-Day Weekend Lifestyle. Now he helps others do it much more quickly.

He's a 20+ year software company founder, business growth coach and author of books that help people grow their businesses, relationships, and finances and live multi-dimensional lives (body, heart, mind, spirit).

He and his family have lived ocean-side in North America and South America.

https://WadeGalt.com

CHAPTER 8

WADE GALT

Why did you join PodMatch as a Podcast Guest member?

I joined PodMatch to connect with high-quality hosts who are actively looking for guests. I don't want to be on as many shows as possible! I want to guest on shows where I can serve my ideal client and people like them. PodMatch is the 80/20 filter for podcast guests & hosts seeking high quality connections without wasting time!

What is one significant way that PodMatch has helped your business/mission?

PodMatch helps me quickly identify high-quality hosts that align with my message. I can:

1) Identify the show's theme.

2) View their website, social media, YouTube, etc., to see if it's high-quality or not.

3) Access and listen to their podcast intro and episodes to evaluate for quality.

4) Identify hosts that do video episodes (which allow for social media video clip assets).

What is your daily routine in PodMatch?

1) I log into PodMatch two-three times per week as a guest to review my matches.

2) I bookmark the best ones and reach out to them with video messages once per month.

3) I reply as quickly as possible to host replies.

What do you recommend as the first thing a new Podcast Guest member should do after joining PodMatch?

Answer these important questions.

1) *What do you hope to accomplish?*

2) *What's the primary solution you want to be known/famous for providing?*

3) *What's the primary message you want to be known/famous for on your episodes?*

4) *What does a perfect outcome/result look like for you when you guest?*

5) *How will you measure success?*

6) *What are your goals?*

7) *What unique gift will you share that listeners can't get anywhere else?*

What do you recommend as the second thing a new Podcast Guest member should do after joining PodMatch?

Put your absolute best foot forward. Create super-high-quality marketing materials.

1) Have a solid website (even if only a few pages).

2) Create your best and clearest PodMatch Profile.

3) Create a compelling PodMatch Video.

4) Create high-quality social media.

5) Share your other podcast guesting links and clips so there's evidence that you'll support the next host's episode.

6) Write LinkedIn recommendations for great hosts (and ask them to do the same).

7) Create solid solo YouTube videos on your channel so hosts can see your work.

8) Launch a podcast, even if only monthly solo episodes. (Hosts LOVE to interview other hosts.)

What "beginner's mistake" did you make with PodMatch that you want to warn other members about?

I wasn't always 100% on time and prepared for my interviews. Now I follow these rules.

1) Be three minutes early and fully hydrated.

2) Restart your computer the same day of your interview. (This reduces software glitches.)

3) Look YOUR best (don't need to be perfect) with a well-lit background, a great mic, and solid Internet connection.

What three PodMatch best practices should every Podcast Guest use regularly?

1) Use PodMatch Pro. This demonstrates you pay for value. Some hosts filter based on this (I do).

2) Follow desired hosts on social media.

3) Do "long-game 'dating' marketing" with desired hosts so they get to know you before you apply. For example:

- Listen to two episodes and write a world class, specific podcast review for them.

- Connect on LinkedIn and share the review there.

- Create a vertical video podcast review and post it on social media.

- Do not ask to be on their show or drop hints in public posts. That puts pressure on them.

What smart tip can you share for any Podcast Guest to use immediately and benefit from?

Follow up like a pro.

Share a social media video after the interview.

"I just completed an interview with _____ from the _____ show, and I'm looking forward to sharing it with you when it's live. In the meanwhile, check out this other episode from the show _____ (link)."

Share the episode when it comes out (on all your active social media). Include the episode links.

Share the screenshot of you recommending their show on iTunes (share on your social media).

Share a social media video when episode releases and tag host. "My interview with _____ just went live. Find it here..." (link).

Comment on and share any episode-related social media posts the host publishes.

Put show links on your website's guesting page.

Share your episode on YouTube.

Offer to introduce them to an awesome guest that fits perfectly with their show.

Write a LinkedIn review for the host. If they respond positively, ask if they'd be open to writing a LinkedIn review for you.

What smart tip can you share to help others get on podcasts where they and their message can have the most impact?

Offer an experience.

1) You are not a product, so don't pitch yourself. You are offering the host a unique experience to serve their audience, learn from you, and ask questions on behalf of their audience (allowing them to be a hero).

2) Create a uniquely recorded video for the host when reaching out to them (e.g., Loom video).

"Here's what I think would serve your audience."

"Here's a title I'm confident would engage your audience" (and tell them why).

"These are the three insights that would most benefit your audience."

"Here's how my message ties into your work and how you can shine" (as the host).

"Here's the gift I'd like to give your audience (with vanity URL)."

"Here's how I share the shows I'm on" (show examples).

3) If you are an author, offer to get the host a paperback, audiobook, or ebook.

What is your final PodMatch "one thing" you want to leave readers with?

Focus on impact to create ROI (return on investment). Apply to guest on shows where you can make a HUGE impact for the audience.

Do not apply to every show unless you want to water down your message and diminish your perceived value. A person who is always available to everyone is (usually accurately) seen as not being a high-value professional.

You will make the biggest impact (and be able to charge the highest income) when you help TRANSFORM an important part of a person's life. Nobody can reach everyone! Even our greatest leaders and spiritual teachers do not appeal to everyone.

Focus on positively changing LIVES (impact), and the income plus unsolicited invitations to be a guest on other shows will eventually follow. The hosts who seek you out will know what you're about, so you won't have to "pitch" yourself. Some hosts will not appear to be a match, but if THEY seek you out, there's often a great (yet to be discovered) reason or connection that can be magical. THAT's when the enjoyment of the process goes to a whole new level. Plus, you get to choose from lots of pre-approved guest opportunities rather than having to seek them out.

Good luck! And enjoy the journey!

Jem Fuller

https://podmatch.com/member/jemfuller

J em Fuller has lived a colourful, global life, from barefoot backpacker to corporate leader, fire-dancer and traditional tattooist, kindergarten teacher to motorcycle courier, masseuse and reflexologist to labourer and travel consultant. Now his time is as partner and father, coach, facilitator and retreat leader. He is the author of the recently published book, *The Art of Conscious Communication for Thoughtful Men*, and can be seen delivering his TEDx talk on YouTube.

https://JemFuller.com

CHAPTER #9

JEM FULLER

Why did you join PodMatch as a Podcast Guest member?

In January of 2022, I was heading out for a run along the cliff-top track above the beach where I live in Australia, and I decided to listen to a random podcast rather than one of the usual shows on my playlist. The guest on the show was a man called, Scott Miller. I loved his energy and decided to reach out to him to connect and see if he had any advice for me. Not only did he email me straight back, but Scott also met me on Zoom and gave generously of his time and wisdom. (We've since become friends and advocates.)

In that very first conversation, one of the pieces of advice he offered was, "Go join PodMatch!" As a recently published author, TEDx speaker and online leadership coach, it was a no-brainer and I joined straight away. Scott had just interviewed Alex Sanfilippo on his "FranklinCovey On Leadership" podcast. He tagged me in a post of Alex's. I felt an alignment, reached out to Alex too, and in our first conversation, we bonded as well.

What is one significant way that PodMatch has helped your business/mission?

My mission is to positively impact lives globally through the sharing of stories and strategies in my books, courses and retreats. Through Pod-Match, in only 6 months of being a member, my interviews have had more than 46,000 listens and more than 1.3 million social impressions! I don't need to employ an expensive podcasting agent to get me spots on good-quality and aligned shows.

There is also a secondary benefit for my business. In my regular newsletters and social posts, my team let our audience and followers know about the latest podcast features that have gone live. This helps build the brand impression of me being "sought after" and in demand.

PodMatch has also provided the entry into a whole new community of like-minded people. I've only been to one of the live events, and had the opportunity to present as a speaker, and it was already massively beneficial. I'm looking forward to deepening the connections I've made and the new ones yet to come.

What is your daily routine in PodMatch?

I log in to PodMatch at the start and end of each day at work. I check my messages and reply to them, scheduling spots on shows that have offered to have me as a guest. Then I check my matches (twice a day) and send a personalized message to show hosts if I feel it would be mutually beneficial for them to have me on. It's important not to ask to be on shows if you don't feel like there is alignment or that you have something to offer their listeners.

What do you recommend as the first thing a new Podcast Guest member should do after joining PodMatch?

Fill out your profile as completely as you can. PodMatch provides so much opportunity for you to showcase yourself and what you can offer to hosts. The platform is so beautifully designed in its functionality. Get the most out of it. ☺

What do you recommend as the second thing a new Podcast Guest member should do after joining PodMatch?

I would jump straight into the educational section and listen to all of the videos that Alex has created to help you get the most out of your membership. There are so many easy user functions I wouldn't have known about without watching those videos.

What "beginner's mistake" did you make with

PodMatch that you want to warn other members about?

When I first joined PodMatch, I was perhaps a little too keen! I was reaching out to every match as soon as they came onto my dashboard, and I was saying yes to every show! I ended up overbooking myself and being interviewed 8–10 times per week. On top of the volume was the time factor. Because I'm in Australia, this meant being online at crazy hours and then still maintaining enough energy for other aspects of my life, like parenting my teenagers and running my business. I've since then developed a more sustainable pace of podcast interviews.

What three PodMatch best practices should every Podcast Guest use regularly?

I'm not sure if these are official PodMatch best practices, but I would certainly encourage users to always:

1) Be respectful. Find out what you can about your host, their show, and their intentions and honour them in your manner and conversation. If you are not OK with what they are about, just don't ask to be a guest on their show.

2) Be timely. Schedule time to check your

messages daily (or have someone do it on your behalf) so that you can reply promptly to any communication.

3) Write reviews. If you feel positive about your experience as a guest, take a few minutes to support your host by writing a review. This really helps them continue to be more successful with their show.

What smart tip can you share for any Podcast Guest to use immediately and benefit from?

This has only happened a few times to me, but when I am getting up at crazy hours in the Australian night to be on a show in the USA or Canada, it's not so great when it happens... "no-shows." Yep, there have been occasions where for one reason or another, I'm sitting there in my studio ready to go, and the host doesn't show up. Eeeek! I don't hold grudges or negative feelings (not my style), but I have learnt to reconfirm appointments 24 hours prior to bookings.

What smart tip can you share to help others get on podcasts where they and their message can have the most impact?

Do your research. Pick the right show with the right audience. This has also been something I have had to get better at. Initially, I was saying yes to almost anyone who would have me on their show. Now I think it's maybe smarter to be on shows with listeners who are at least open to what I'm offering. My approach was very altruistic, just wanting to have good quality conversations with good people and hopefully share some insights that might help even one listener. I think perhaps it still is to some degree. I still don't ask how successful the show is, how big the audience or how many downloads. I want to do my bit to support even smaller podcasts. Perhaps one day my business manager will intervene and ask me to be more selective with my limited time? Who knows.

What is your final PodMatch "one thing" you want to leave readers with?

I have only just recently learnt to have a specific call-to-action. I was just sending people to my website or socials, but now I ask hosts prior to the show if they are OK with me offering their listeners a coupon code as a gift to one of my online courses. I haven't had anyone say "no" yet.

As much as we are serving the greater good, we are also serving the higher purpose of our own mission. We need to let people know how they can get more of what we have to offer.

Jem Fuller

Steve Lowell

https://podmatch.com/member/stevelowell

Steve Lowell is a multi-award-winning speaker, three-time #1 best-selling author, and master trainer for high-impact speakers with a track record that speaks for itself. Having given over 3,500 keynote speeches, 5,000 seminars, and trained more than 500K speakers globally, Steve delivers innovative strategies that help speakers, coaches, consultants and experts of all kinds to drive revenue from the stage and build wealth through speaking.

Steve has been on the live stage since the age of 6; that's over 50 years of experience! He is a master at helping aspiring and elite speakers develop the platform skills and delivery techniques they need to truly deliver a transformational message that translates to revenue.

https://SteveLowell.com

CHAPTER #10

STEVE LOWELL

Why did you join PodMatch as a Podcast Guest member?

I decided that being a guest on podcasts would be a good way to drive traffic to my evergreen webinars, but I had no idea where to find the right podcasts.

I tried searching for podcasts that might fit, but it was so hard to sift through the millions of podcasts that are out there and find the ones that might work for me. And even then, I had no idea how to contact the hosts of those podcasts or how to approach it. Then I found PodMatch.

What is one significant way that PodMatch has helped your business/mission?

Once I found PodMatch and started booking some guest spots, I learned that my original expectations of podcasting were not realistic. My expectations were that I would be a guest on a podcast and then sit back and watch the traffic to my webinar traffic go up. Well, it seems that I was being a little naive!

I soon discovered that the power of being a guest on podcasts does not always come from the audience they reach but from the hosts themselves. I call it "connection equity."

Because of PodMatch, I was able to be a guest on many podcasts where I made great connections with those podcast hosts. They, in turn, were happy to introduce me to other hosts who also booked me as a guest. Some of those hosts have become joint-venture partners and even clients.

As one who makes a living speaking at conventions and conferences, I have known that the most valuable part of almost every conference is the connections we make in the halls or at the bar. I learned that the same holds true, at least for me, in the podcast world. The best value has been the connection equity.

Has my traffic to my webinar increased? Probably not by much, but I do get messages from people who have heard me on different podcasts and want to connect with me and speak with me. As a result, I have made some great, new connections, affiliated with some strong joint-venture partners and signed up a few clients along the way.

What is your daily routine in PodMatch?

I don't really have a daily routine in PodMatch. I go into PodMatch when I'm ready to explore more matches. I always know that I can drop in, find a handful of matches, and start working those. PodMatch is like the ATM for podcast guests (and hosts too).

What do you recommend as the first thing a new Podcast Guest member should do after joining PodMatch?

The very first thing I did when I joined PodMatch was to start clicking. My recommendation to a new guest member would be to click, click and click, and get a feel for where things are.

Read everything that pops up and get oriented inside the system. The reason I think this is important is because you'll get to know if you feel at home inside the system or not. Once I get a sense as to how I feel about the environment, then I decide if I'm going to stay or not. Then I move to the next recommendation.

What do you recommend as the second thing a new Podcast Guest member should do after joining PodMatch?

Make sure you're ready to go.

Once you have oriented yourself with the environment, the next step is to review all the mini training videos so you can understand how PodMatch works.

There's much more to PodMatch than meets the eye. You should understand how the whole thing works before you go further because there are some tips in those training videos that will inform how you proceed.

Earlier I mentioned that I like to navigate the entire site before I get the training. I do this so I will already be familiar with the references in the training videos. This is how it all makes sense to me.

You need to be properly prepared before you start making connections. These training videos will help you get ready.

You may get some matches who would like you on their show three months in the future. But you'll also find some who have an opening right now, and you need to be ready when that happens.

Aside from having your profile all set up and all the other obvious things, you do need to know how to maneuver through the processes when you do make connections, and that can begin very quickly.

What "beginner's mistake" did you make with PodMatch that you want to warn other members about?

I made two mistakes when I started with Pod-Match.

The first mistake was thinking I was every host's dream guest. Imagine my surprise when I reached out to a potential match and they said, "No thank you."

I needed to understand that some podcast hosts have a specific focus and desired outcome for their podcasts, and although my topic may seem to be in alignment on the surface, it might not align to the desired outcomes of some of the hosts, and that's OK.

The second mistake was to get intimidated by the analytics that are provided by the podcast hosts. The hosts of the podcasts want the best possible guests; that only makes sense. So, they want their podcast to be appealing to potential guests. One way they do that is with the analytics information they include in their PodMatch profile.

I would look at some of the huge numbers of downloads and hundreds of episodes and I would sometimes hesitate to reach out to those hosts because I felt like they wouldn't be interested in me. That was a mistake!

After a very short time, I was speaking on three and sometimes four podcasts every single day for weeks at a time. I actually had to pull back because I need to run my business.

What three PodMatch best practices should every Podcast Guest use regularly?

There are a few obvious things you need to do regularly, like check your matches and your inbox. Here are some less obvious things to do:

1) Review your profile regularly. As you appear on more podcasts, you'll get to know what podcast hosts like and what they look for. So, updating your profile to highlight those things which attract the podcast hosts the most is a good way to stay top of mind and top of the search results!

2) Review your list of pre-suggested questions. After you have answered your selected questions a few times, you may notice that there are questions that don't best serve you or questions to which you may not like your own answers. Reviewing your questions will help keep your interviews aligned to your goals for being a guest in the first place.

3) Do more interviews; get GOOD at it!

What smart tip can you share for any Podcast Guest to use immediately and benefit from?

Memorize and use these words with every podcast host just before you say goodbye: *"Who else do you know?"*

Find out from them who else they know who has a podcast or who might be a possible alliance for you, and then ask them to make an introduction. This one technique alone can skyrocket your connection equity.

What smart tip can you share to help others get on podcasts where they and their message can have the most impact?

There's no secret here. Just do it! Enough with hesitation, procrastination, and excuses. Just get logged in and get it done.

What is your final PodMatch "one thing" you want to leave readers with?

Podcasting is like speaking. It's not about transferring information; it's about transferring emotion. If you can get your audience to feel about your message the way YOU feel about your message, now you have communication.

John & Mark Cronin

https://podmatch.com/member/markxcronin

John and Mark X. Cronin are the father-son team that created John's Crazy Socks, a social enterprise with a mission to spread happiness. They bootstrapped their start up into a multi-million-dollar business that has become the world's largest sock store and an international sensation.

John is not only a business owner, but he also has Down syndrome. Every day, John and Mark show what people with differing abilities can do—more than half their colleagues have a differing ability. Their Giving Back program has raised over $500,000 for their charity partners, like the Special Olympics. Their advocacy work has seen them testify twice before Congress and speak at the United Nations. They are keynote speakers and have been featured on multiple national news programs. And their commitment to customer experience has earned them fiercely loyal customers.

https://JohnsCrazySocks.com

JOHN & MARK CRONIN

Why did you join PodMatch as a Podcast Guest member?

Once we determined that we wanted to appear on podcasts as a guest, we needed to find the right podcasts for us. PodMatch fit the bill in two ways. First, it allowed us to put ourselves out there as potential guests. Second, it not only allowed us to find podcasts looking for guests, but it also allowed us to find the right podcasts for our story and message.

What is one significant way that PodMatch has helped your business/mission?

Our business, John's Crazy Socks, is a social enterprise with a mission to spread happiness. Much of that mission involves showing what people with differing abilities can do. My partner and son, John, has Down syndrome, and it was his idea to start this business. We have bootstrapped the business into the largest sock store in the world. At the end of the day, we are not really a sock store; yes, we have more socks than anyone else and people love the products—we have over 30,000 five-star reviews—but the socks are the physical manifestation of our story and our mission.

Appearing as podcast guests has allowed us to tell our story and to reach new audiences. In the past 12 months, we have appeared on well over 100 podcasts. This has allowed us to meet wonderful hosts and to reach new audiences, and that allows us to pursue our mission of spreading happiness and showing what people with differing abilities can achieve.

PodMatch has enabled us to find the podcasts that are right for us. There are approximately one gazillion podcasts out there, but not all are a good fit for us. PodMatch helps us find the podcasts where we will be the best match for the hosts and the audiences.

What is your daily routine in PodMatch?

For many months, I managed our PodMatch listing, and then my colleague, Maria, who is our Community Organizer, took over. Maria takes the lead in booking us on podcasts and making sure that we provide the host with all the necessary information in advance to make their jobs easier.

Maria follows the same routine that I did. We check to see if there are any messages on Pod-Match. We will then check to see if there are any recommended matches. If there are, we decide if we want to pursue the matches. If we do, we reach out to those podcasts.

What do you recommend as the first thing a new Podcast Guest member should do after joining PodMatch?

Our first step was to complete the profile on PodMatch so that others could find us and understand what we were about. That gave hosts the best opportunity to see if we would be a good match for them.

What do you recommend as the second thing a new Podcast Guest member should do after joining PodMatch?

Very quickly, we realized that we needed to create an email introducing us to a podcast's host and explaining why we would be a good fit for that podcast. We actually created a set of templates emphasizing different points that would meet the interests of the podcast host and audience. For example, we have one for a podcast aimed at entrepreneurs, one for a podcast aimed at parenting and so on. We then personalize each template for the specific podcast.

Once we heard back from a podcast, we prepared a package of information to provide them with an opportunity to learn more about us and also help them prepare for the podcast interview. We assembled a Guest Podcast Kit with the following materials:

- A One Sheet describing John and me as podcast guests. (We almost always appear together.) That One Sheet provides an overview and bio, media appearances, topics we can discuss and more (see it on page 150).

- A document with helpful information, including links to our website and social media sites, links to our TEDx talks, links to intro videos, lists of media appearances and more information.

- Bios and an introduction.

- Headshots.

We also prepared a set of email templates that we then tailor for the specific podcast:

- One that provided the Guest Podcast Kit.

- One that offered to promote the podcasts on our social media platforms and website.

- One that offered other ways we could help the podcasts, e.g., discount code, box of socks for use in a contest, etc.

- One that made them aware of business services we could offer that might help, e.g., custom socks, gift packages, etc.

We also prepared a follow-up email thanking the host and asking if there is anything we can do to help.

We found that making the investment of time to set up these templates made everything easier, and it helps us communicate with the podcast host. We want to give the host everything he or she needs to learn about us and to interview us. And we want to help promote the podcast.

What "beginner's mistake" did you make with PodMatch that you want to warn other members about?

When I started with PodMatch, I was too disorganized and too scattershot. I did not check every day, so I would spend hours on one day and no time the next few days. I also created a new intro email every time I reached out to a podcast.

Once I settled down into a routine and we created our standard documents, everything became easier and more effective.

What smart tip can you share for any Podcast Guest to use immediately and benefit from?

Prepare the Guest Podcast Kit. It will make things easier for you and make a great impression on the podcast host.

What smart tip can you share to help others get on podcasts where they and their message can have the most impact?

Find the podcasts that reach audiences that make sense for you. We set a monthly target on the number of podcasts on which we would appear. One danger is spending time on podcasts that are not a good fit. Starting out, we did not worry about reach, but we did want to make sure we aligned with the subject matter and approach of the host.

What is your final PodMatch "one thing" you want to leave readers with?

Appearing as guests on podcasts has been important to our growth. It is a perfect format to tell our story and to reach new audiences in a personal way. We just returned from a speaking engagement at a conference in Fargo, North Dakota. The person who hired us first heard us on a podcast. That is an example of how podcasts have worked for us.

John and Mark Cronin

Amy Scruggs

Amy Scruggs is known in country music for more than 15 years opening for greats, including Clint Black, Trace Adkins, and many more. She was the spokesperson for the AMVETS Department of California 2009-2011.

Amy's career also includes 20 years in sales team coaching and received Bestseller on her book, *Lights Camera Action*, in 2021. The past 5 years, she enjoyed her position as TV host for *The American Dream* on CNBC and several other shows.

Amy uses her experience as a media executive, TV host, recording artist, and public speaker to help others communicate a concise and professional message for network TV, podcast, social media or in-person public speaking appearances.

Her new single released in 2022, "What If It All Goes Right," is on radio worldwide.

https://AmyScruggsMedia.com

CHAPTER #12

AMY SCRUGGS

Why did you join PodMatch as a Podcast Guest member?

Spending years as a TV host gave me the love for the interviewing process. I have had extensive experience as a guest and as a host on various media platforms and love each opportunity to expand my network and visibility along with creating the ability to grow in my skills as a guest. I knew joining PodMatch was going to create new strategic relationship-building and promotion opportunities.

What is one significant way that PodMatch has helped your business/mission?

PodMatch interviews have introduced me to other incredible professionals that are aligned strategically with my business and entrepreneur values. This creates new collaborating opportunities outside of the already valuable visibility that the podcasts provide.

What is your daily routine in PodMatch?

I check my PodMatch account every day and respond to any messages in the inbox. I then go through my dashboard for any items that need my attention and review any upcoming podcasts for the week to familiarize myself with those hosts and shows. The next step I enjoy as I review the matches to strategically check each one and select the best-fitting shows for putting in a request to be a guest. I personalize my private message to each one so that it reflects my interest for being a guest with the topic that is also the best fit for their unique show.

What do you recommend as the first thing a new Podcast Guest member should do after joining PodMatch?

Completing the individual profile is the most important beginning strategy for a new member. This profile needs to share a complete and concise overview of each member and their specialty and best topics. If the profile is not rich in content and attractive to hosts, then maximizing the great value of PodMatch will be harder to achieve. I personally look at every profile of the hosts that I am reaching out to, and if the links don't work or there is only slight information on the show, then I pass on the match. As a guest, I know that my profile needs to be complete and first class to attract the top-quality shows along with the right shows for my expertise and business.

What do you recommend as the second thing a new Podcast Guest member should do after joining PodMatch

Once a new member has a full profile, it is time to have fun with the matches that come in every day. It is a great opportunity to explore and put yourself out there to the hosts to start filling up the interviewing calendar. Start the process of getting booked on shows and finding out how to work the platform, engaging with the hosts and the follow-up after. This will be beneficial for the increased opportunity for relationships and networking. The more "asks" you put out there, the better the chances for continued success. Besides the recommended matches on the platform, it is fun to go and explore to find out what shows are out there in the categories that fit you as a guest. I love finding new shows that didn't come into my daily matches and asking for the interview.

What "beginner's mistake" did you make with PodMatch that you want to warn other members about?

At the beginning, I was not going on twice a day to take advantage of all the matches. I started with once a day and realized I was missing opportunities for more shows along with helping my matches to become increasingly more accurate to my specific topics and business.

I also noticed that I still had more details I could add to my profile to make it thorough and attractive to great show hosts. Since I have created the daily habits and profile updates as needed, I have noticed an increase in my accurate matches and the quality of shows that I am booking.

What three PodMatch best practices should every Podcast Guest use regularly?

Practice, daily discipline and follow-up!!

It starts with the practice of strategic talking points, messaging, branding, and storytelling for a great interview experience for all.

Second, is the daily discipline of being in the PodMatch platform and using the booking and communications tools provided.

The third most important is the follow-up with the hosts. Let them know that you are looking forward to the interview and that you are confirming your time slot by reaching them on email or in the messages area. After the show, send a thank you, engage on social media, share the content, and always do a review. These new relationships with the hosts can create great networking and future collaborations.

What smart tip can you share for any Podcast Guest to use immediately and benefit from?

Thank the host before, during and after the show for having you on their platform. Exhibit professionalism and respect in how you communicate and value their time as professionals. Listen to an episode of their show prior to your interview as well so that you have a feel for their hosting style, questions and flow.

What smart tip can you share to help others get on podcasts where they and their message can have the most impact?

Creating brief strategic talking points, buzz words and show topics that could be ready to present in the message is a great way to personalize the asking process. It shows the host that you took the time to understand their specific show platform and how you will bring value to their show through your expertise and knowledge.

What is your final PodMatch "one thing" you want to leave readers with?

It is so important to take the time to know your specific individual story and talking points. Going into an interview and starting off the dialogue with "*Um, ya, uhh, or sooo*" shows that the preparation and self-awareness are not ready for being a guest. The host wants to know that their show is going to be engaging and full of great information and energy.

The preparation of being a guest is worth its weight in gold. Practicing is the key. It makes sense to know your personal 20-minute, 30-minute, or 1-hour story that will adapt to any show.

Being an author with a great book or running a successful business are different skills than learning how to effectively communicate in an interview setting. There is a lot of preparation that goes into place with knowing the strategic talking points of your story and using great active listening skills so that you follow your host and adapt as it goes along.

An effective way of evaluating how your first interviews delivered is by going back and watching and listening to the shows. Listen from the perspective of the audience. Take notes on what you noticed were great talking points and sound bites and what parts maybe took too long to get to the main point.

Was there good energy?

Was there good interaction with the host?

Did it bring value to the listener?

These are key components to mastering the guest interviewing process and getting booked on future shows.

Daniel Alfon

D aniel Alfon is the author of *Build a LinkedIn Profile for Business Success*. Daniel joined LinkedIn in early 2004, which means he has made all the mistakes you can imagine but came back to tell what works!

Today, Daniel's clients get results organically: No need to spam people when growing your business. Absolutely no need to share 24/7 when pivoting. And you never have to become someone else, because LinkedIn is here to serve you and not the other way around.

Daniel publishes articles, interviews and exclusive content about advanced LinkedIn strategies for clients and subscribers on his website:

https://DanielAlfon.com

CHAPTER 13

DANIEL ALFON

Why did you join PodMatch as a Podcast Guest member?

Curiosity. If my journey could be described like the days of the week, here's how it'd look:

Sunday: "Let's just see if any host really says yes."

Monday: "We could do this unscripted?"

Tuesday: "Wot! With video? Wow!"

Wednesday: "Live? You mean really live?"

Thursday: "Other guests, like a panel?"

Friday: "Hosts from different cultures! Whoa!"

Saturday: "(Sigh) Daddy, how did you live prior to PodMatch or electricity?"

If it weren't for PodMatch, I would never have considered being a guest on podcasts. Naturally, when PodMatch landed me my first podcast recordings, I got "curiouser and curiouser" and became a paying member. *Who wouldn't?*

But why do I stay?

- Thought leadership: The About section of my website, DanielAlfon.com, now looks like Around the World in 80 Podcasts. US hosts are featured next to flags from Canada, UK, Australia, India, South Africa, France, Poland, Brazil, Singapore and Germany—with Jordan, New Zealand and Hong Kong being added soon.

- Becoming a pro guest: The variety—LinkedIn Live, YouTube Premiere, Facebook Live livestreaming as well as StreamYard, Discord, Zoom/Meet/Teams, audio—makes you sharpen your toolbox and further customize your message.

- Networking: I met a-m-a-z-i-n-g hosts.

What is one significant way that PodMatch has helped your business/mission?

Recent invitations to keynotes, webinars, summits, stages and podcasts (duh) that I landed happened chiefly thanks to PodMatch-enabled bookings. My presentations are getting better because I now read *Superior Presentations* by George Torok (whom I met on PodMatch). Moreover, all visitors to my website now see a wealth of shows. This helped my website's ranking, which in turn, leads to new opportunities.

What is your daily routine in PodMatch?

Checking incoming requests, catching up with messages, reviewing new matches, deciding to accept match/pitch, and scheduling. Preparing today's recording/pre-recording chat. Sharing/commenting on released episodes.

What do you recommend as the first thing a new Podcast Guest member should do after joining PodMatch?

Option 1: Wing it, waste time, whine and leave.

Option 2: Start by completing the PodMatch Education (Checklist). Watch the first video, take notes, implement, and then move to the next video. Book podcasts.

Pro tip: Option 2 will save you a ton of time.

What do you recommend as the second thing a new Podcast Guest member should do after joining PodMatch?

Optimizing your Guest Profile. I've witnessed the benefits of a converting profile.

What "beginner's mistake" did you make with PodMatch that you want to warn other members about?

I pitched (poorly) to all matches, instead of passing and focusing on the best matches and preparing them thoroughly.

What three PodMatch best practices should every Podcast Guest use regularly?

1) Prior to the interview:

Decide whether you pitch/confirm the match based on the right criteria (target audience rather than downloads). Listen to interesting recent episodes (Scripted or freestyle? Recorded or Live?). Submit (tweaked?) bio/headshot/ answers/social links/form exactly like the host requested. Make sure PodMatch reflects the actual recording date. Pin unscheduled/VIP hosts. Follow host on social. Rate the show on Apple/Spotify®. Make sure your calendar shows the right time in your time zone, with StreamYard/Zoom link. Verify that you have the host's email/number. Research! Prepare specific examples for the show's audience. If you don't have a link, reach out before recording and politely ask when you should expect it.

2) When recording:

Show up on time. Clean your mind and desk [notifications off, phones muted]. Use headphones and an external microphone. Listen carefully. Use the pre-recording time to build rapport. Thank the host's team. Ask any outstanding questions you may have (Can I share my screen? What would make a great episode?).

Surprise your host in a positive way, by research-ing them. Find a way to mention the host's work —a previous guest they interviewed, a recent tweet, etc.

3) After recording:

Stay after recording ends. Let the host speak first. Ask for feedback and listen carefully. When possible, ask who'd be a good guest on the show, and if the host would like to be a guest on other people's shows, what podcasts would they like to be a guest on. Understand the estimated release date. Add it to a calendar-based system. After 24 hours, mark recording as complete on PodMatch. Rate the host on PodMatch to help the team. See how you can help the host. When it's live, listen to your episode! Tag/share/like on your channels, website and email list. Personally thank the host (email). When sharing on LinkedIn: Tag the host. Instead of just dropping the link, make the effort to quote an interesting question, a funny incident that got recorded, the host's website or program, or previous guests. If the host shared the episode, comment in a meaningful way, trying to make the conversation open-ended by asking a question.

What smart tip can you share for any Podcast Guest to use immediately and benefit from?

Log in regularly, and customize your pitch (for paying members: create a video pitch)!

What smart tip can you share to help others get on podcasts where they and their message can have the most impact?

Follow/attend PodMatch events (quarterly, summits...) to become a better guest; follow Alex & PodPros to catch the latest from podcasters.

What is your final PodMatch "one thing" you want to leave readers with?

The guest who does the following? #Don'tBeThatGuest:

- (cough) ...re we on? (spit) I've been on this YardStream for 10 minutes, man.

- EST? No way. I never record in EST, this is like...New York time. You must have gotten it all backwards, that was 3 hours ago.

- Well, I'm here now, ain't I? Let's record this (mumbling: my name alone will bring you 10x downloads, you mo---).

- I don't recall any online form with requests I submitted.

- Bio? I'll introduce myself then: "Matthew Lightstone is God's gift to Human---" (angrily:) What NOW?

- HONEY? CAN YOU DO THOSE DISHES LATER? Says there's background noise so we have to start over. Can you take the kiddos to the park so I can concentrate around here?

- iPhones? Oh, EARphones! You're not clear, dude. Yeah, I can see you have 'em. ME? I no longer use them. They were worthless really...

- Now why would I turn the darn camera on? I thought this was pure audio.

- It's over! Say, when does the episode drop? Gotta feed it to my fans, y'know?

- Live WHAT? You mean we were live this whole time?? Why so many comments, did they love my style? No, it's not the first time I trend on Twitter. I'm hot! Quick, what hashtag? #Don'tBeThatGuest?

- See? That's what happens when hosts are such AMATEURS!!!

Peter George

https://podmatch.com/member/petergeorge

Peter is a public speaking coach, speaker, TEDx coach, and author. For nearly two decades, he has helped people develop dynamic public speaking skills. As a result, they can consistently and confidently deliver compelling presentations that resonate with and benefit their audiences. To help people achieve this, he created the AMP'D Framework™. It's an easy-to-follow system based on the magical blend of art and science that produces engaging talks and captivating speakers.

A highly sought-after speaker, Peter has spoken to audiences in seven countries—more than 50 countries when including virtual formats.

Peter is the author of *The Captivating Speaker: Engage, Impact, and Inspire Your Audience Every Time*. He is also the host of the "Public Speaking with Peter George" podcast.

CHAPTER 14

PETER GEORGE

Why did you join PodMatch as a Podcast Guest member?

When I decided to be a guest on podcasts, I spent an inordinate amount of time searching the web, Apple Podcasts, Spotify®, and the like for shows that focused on public speaking. I had some success but not enough to consider my effort worthwhile. Then I learned about PodMatch.

PodMatch not only made locating appropriate podcasts much easier, but it also helped me achieve a much higher success rate when contacting prospective shows. As a result, I made many more connections with other professionals related to my field, got greater exposure, and actually enjoyed reaching out to hosts.

What is one significant way that PodMatch has helped your business/mission?

Surveys show that the number one reason businesses fail is lack of funds. I have no reason to doubt this. But I believe another reason that must rank near the top is obscurity. When companies, especially small companies, attempt to gain the exposure necessary to thrive, they have to turn to their inadequate funding. The answer, of course, is to gain exposure through highly cost-effective means. And that is precisely what PodMatch has done for me.

I have been a speaker for over 35 years and a speaking coach for nearly 20 years, so I am relatively well recognized in certain areas. However, there are many targeted areas where I still have work to do. This is especially true when it comes to publicizing my new book, *The Captivating Speaker: Engage, Impact, and Inspire Your Audience Every Time*. By being a frequent guest on podcasts, I have gained added exposure and steadily increased the number of books sold.

What is your daily routine in PodMatch?

As a guest, I use PodMatch weekly, which fits into my routine and serves me well. During this time, I follow a fairly consistent process.

1) Review the Dashboard. This helps ensure that the hosts I have connected with and I get the most from the system and experience.

2) Answer inquiries from those who would like me to be a guest on their shows.

3) Follow up with hosts after initially connecting with them or being a guest.

4) Explore shows where I would be a good fit.

I can't imagine how long all this would take without the PodMatch system. But because the system is easy to navigate, my time there is spent efficiently and effectively, increasing my success and enjoyment.

What do you recommend as the first thing a new Podcast Guest member should do after joining PodMatch?

Without a doubt, the first thing you should do is watch the educational videos. To be honest, I didn't watch them at first. Instead, I checked things out on my own—clicking on this button and that link, seeing what each one did. Then I learned that you get credit towards your ranking on the leaderboard when completing the videos. Being competitive, I had to watch the videos. So, I played them but without really paying attention.

Then one day, while on indefinite hold with a service provider, I truly listened to one of the videos and found the information more than helpful. Immediately, I went back and watched the others. When I was done, I wished I had watched them sooner. The short time it takes to view them delivers a return on your investment many times over.

What do you recommend as the second thing a new Podcast Guest member should do after joining PodMatch?

The second thing I suggest is that you put time into your Guest Profile page. It's here that hosts will determine if you will be a good fit for their shows.

When you are completing this profile, be specific! The more specific you are, the more likely the right hosts will contact you.

If completing your Guest Profile sounds daunting, don't worry. Each section guides you along. I suggest you also look at the pages of successful guests and emulate them. Although you want this page to be helpful to you and your potential hosts, please do not overthink this initially. You can always go back and edit it.

What "beginner's mistake" did you make with PodMatch that you want to warn other members about?

Aside from not watching the educational videos right away, another mistake I made was not thoroughly researching shows before reaching out to the hosts. This mistake often led to being rejected and was a waste of the hosts' and my time.

Although you may be tempted to contact as many hosts as possible while doing little more than reading their podcast profiles, you will save yourself time, increase your success rate, and reduce frustration by carefully researching each show before deciding to contact the host.

What three PodMatch best practices should every Podcast Guest use regularly?

1) The #1 practice you should use regularly is to show up! Nothing is more exasperating to a host than to be waiting for a guest to show up and they don't. Failing to show up or canceling at the last minute is neither professional nor respectful. Hosts under-stand that emergencies happen. But unless it is truly an emergency, show up as sched-uled.

2) When you show up, be prepared. Some-times, depending on when your availability coincides with the host's, it may be a while before you record your interview. When this is the case (even when it isn't), review the topic you agreed on and any other particu-

lars. Then, listen again to an episode or two. The recording may live in perpetuity, so even though it doesn't have to be perfect, you want to represent yourself and the host as well as possible.

3) Be concise and interactive. Hosts and audiences dread a guest droning on and on. Sure, some answers might require a little more time than others, but don't make long answers a habit. While answering the host's questions, you can occasionally ask the host a question. Also, remember to use the host's name and acknowledge their audience.

What smart tip can you share for any Podcast Guest to use immediately and benefit from?

Immediately after scheduling an interview, send the host the information they may need. This information includes your name, company name (if applicable), contact info, brief bio, social media links, and anything else you think appropriate without bombarding them with unnecessary details. Along with this, send a headshot and other images, such as your logo, product, etc.

By sending these immediately after booking your interview, you provide the host with the information they may need and demonstrate your professionalism and respect.

What smart tip can you share to help others get on podcasts where they and their message can have the most impact?

This idea might seem trivial, but it's not! Have one call-to-action. When hosts ask guests where their listeners can connect with them, guests often provide a litany of options. This can be confusing to listeners. Instead, provide only one. This call-to-action might be for the listeners to go to your website. It could be asking the listeners to connect with you on one of your social media pages. It might be to have them go to Amazon and order your book. In any case, if you want the host's listeners to take action, provide just one directive.

What is your final PodMatch "one thing" you want to leave readers with?

Alex and the team at PodMatch have created a superb platform that helps you connect with podcasts where you can provide value to their listeners. However, the key to this platform is you. Put the time and effort into it, and you will prosper.

Jason Cercone

https://podmatch.com/member/jasoncercone

Jason Cercone is a personal brand architect, creator, and podcaster. He helps entrepreneurs, leaders, and professionals leverage the brand-building power of the podcast medium to establish authority, increase visibility, and accelerate the evolution of their personal brand.

Positioning yourself as a compelling, value-driven podcast guest allows you to make an impact with each and every appearance you make, but it's important to understand how to be an asset to podcasters, establish lucrative relationships, and maximize each opportunity you have so real, tangible growth can be experienced. Jason specializes in helping you tap into your authentic brand story and how to share it with clarity, confidence, and consistency on podcasts that align with your objectives.

He is also the host of the "Evolution of Brand" podcast.

https://JasonCercone.com

CHAPTER 15

JASON CERCONE

Why did you join PodMatch as a Podcast Guest member?

When I signed up for PodMatch, I discovered quickly how easy it was to connect with like-minded professionals in the podcast space. My first step was to communicate with potential guests for my podcast, and before I knew it...my calendar was booked to the point that I was able to expand my weekly episode releases!

I knew I had struck gold and immediately began reaching out to other podcasts and generating guest appearances for myself.

My specialty is helping entrepreneurs, coaches, and professionals build their personal brand as podcast guests. So naturally, my primary branding initiative is bringing value to other podcasts as a compelling, engaging guest. PodMatch makes it easy to discover, connect, and plan collaborations with fellow podcasters across the globe!

What is one significant way that PodMatch has helped your business/mission?

Without question, the greatest gift PodMatch has given me is a stronger, healthier network. It's hard for me to capture in words the impact those I've collaborated with have had on my life, both professionally and personally. I've been able to reach a much larger audience by guesting on relevant podcasts. I've gained business from those guest appearances, made new friends and business relationships, and my knowledge base has expanded immensely thanks to the powerful conversations I've had.

What is your daily routine in PodMatch?

I block 30 minutes two times a day to answer any incoming messages I've received for guest opportunities as well as other professionals looking to join me on my podcast. In that time, I also check my PodMatch-generated matches and do some additional targeted searches for podcasts that fall into my area of expertise. As a baseline, I try to connect with five podcasters a day via the Pod-Match platform. I'm a firm believer in playing the numbers game. The more connections you make, the more opportunities you create for guest opportunities.

What do you recommend as the first thing a new Podcast Guest member should do after joining PodMatch?

Build a captivating profile that "tells someone the time but doesn't build them a watch." What I mean by that is brevity is your friend. A profile that has every single detail about you can be tough to consume. Think of your Guest Profile like a movie trailer. A trailer doesn't give away the whole movie. It shares a few minutes of scenes to get you amped to see the full movie. Your profile should serve the same purpose. Hit the highlights, and inspire someone to reach out to you and start a conversation to learn more about you.

What do you recommend as the second thing a new Podcast Guest member should do after joining PodMatch?

Don't waste any time. Start making connections as soon as possible and experience the gains PodMatch will bring to your efforts.

A helpful tip: Be genuine with your correspondences, and don't send lengthy outreach messages. Take a few minutes to look at the podcast's profile, make sure it's a good fit, listen to some content, and connect with a friendly message designed to start a conversation. Don't oversell... let your value speak for itself!

What "beginner's mistake" did you make with PodMatch that you want to warn other members about?

Do not get upset or question your decision to join PodMatch if a podcaster chooses not to match and collaborate with you. You cannot control whether a podcaster feels you're a good match. You can only control the value you bring to the microphone, and I guarantee you will discover podcasters that recognize your value and want to put it center stage on their show. Keep making connections on a consistent basis, and your dance card will be booked before you know it.

Additionally, don't get frustrated if someone doesn't respond right away. Some members don't check their profiles frequently. Some will see your message and not respond at all. Again, these are items you cannot control. It doesn't hurt to follow up with someone if they don't respond, but don't let it consume you. PodMatch is a flourishing community with thousands of people for you to meet. Approach it with an abundance mindset, and everything will fall into place.

What three PodMatch best practices should every Podcast Guest use regularly?

1) Keep the lines of communications open before, during, and after each and every

guest appearance with the podcast host and their team. Remember, the interview is just one piece of the puzzle. Your ability to network and establish strong, lucrative relationships is equally as valuable to the podcast guest experience.

2) PodMatch allows you to list suggested questions designed to help podcasters build interview formats that cater to your expertise. Use this feature to provide dynamic, compelling questions that go a few layers beneath the surface and stimulate riveting conversations when a podcaster serves them up to you. The more engaging the conversation, the more people will want to listen.

3) Always leave a rating and written review for every podcast you appear on. Ratings and reviews not only give listeners an idea of what a show is about, they also help podcasts get discovered. Since it's a given that you want more people to find a podcast and hear your message, take two minutes to leave some positive feedback.

What smart tip can you share for any Podcast Guest to use immediately and benefit from?

Do not use the podcast platform to go into sales mode. Put yourself in the position of the listener.

When you hit play on a podcast, do you want to hear a compelling conversation that teaches you something new, helps you solve a problem, and provides you with an entertaining escape from your world..., or do you want to hear an infomercial that tries to sell you something from start to finish?

The vast majority of podcast listeners prefer the latter, so check the overbearing sales shtick at the door. Instead, use your guest appearances to provide value, showcase your expertise, and give listeners a reason to seek you out for even more value once the episode concludes.

When you proceed in this fashion, the host will do the selling for you! Because you delivered and helped them create quality content that will help them grow their audience, they'll emphatically tell their listeners why they need to invest in your brand.

In other words, being a value-driven podcast guest allows you to sell without actually selling.

What smart tip can you share to help others get on podcasts where they and their message can have the most impact?

Root all of your efforts in value, and treat each podcaster you approach with the respect they deserve. Like you, they have an objective. They're on a mission to create quality content that makes their content recommendable, thus fueling audience growth that could open up a world of opportunity.

As the guest, you play a key role in the creation of that content. The more you understand what the podcaster wants to accomplish and how your expertise will help them accomplish it, the better the chemistry will be when your interview begins and the more dynamic the final product will be for people to consume.

When everyone works collectively and focuses on helping each other instead of just completing a transaction, everyone—the host, the guest, and the audience—wins.

What is your final PodMatch "one thing" you want to leave readers with?

Positive results are born from consistency and authenticity.

Just like everything you do to build your brand, your efforts within PodMatch will be rewarded if you do things consistently and simply be yourself. This will lead to more engaging conversations, better results, and relationships that could last a lifetime.

Vinnie Potestivo

https://podmatch.com/member/vinniepotestivo

Vinnie is an Emmy® Award-winning media advisor who helps clients leverage their media exposure, find fame, and make impact.

As TV network talent executive at MTV Networks (98-07), he pioneered the way brands and business owners could contribute to their public narrative by making them stars and producers of their own television series. Early hits include *Punk'd, The Osbournes, TRL, 8th & Ocean, Wild 'N Out*, and *The Challenge*. He and his team at VPE.tv have become well-trusted connectors who develop and distribute original content across all media platforms.

As the editor-in-chief of ihaveapodcast.com, he amplifies the voice of independent podcast talent in addition to dissecting the creative process with the stars and creatives who helped launch his career, such as Mandy Moore, Danielle Fishel, and Ananda Lewis on "I Have A Podcast." Want access? Tune in now:

https://IHaveaPodcast.com

CHAPTER 16

VINNIE POTESTIVO

Why did you join PodMatch as a Podcast Guest member?

To use dating as a metaphor: I jumped around and "dated" many other podcast matchmaking sites until I ultimately met my match with Pod-Match. Let's be honest; I kept it casual because I never felt fulfilled. Pitch after pitch, it started to feel like I was talking into thin air. I had no chemistry. I thought it was me until I met Pod-Match, and then it was love at first sight, or should I say last site.

More than any other guest-booking website, I found PodMatch podcasters were more attentive to receiving pitches, which made it much easier to book (and start scaling) my podcast guest-appearance strategy. Attentive, reactive, and quick to take action are great qualities to look for in a podcast collaboration.

I also love that PodMatch doesn't require you to search for podcasts and message them blindly. Instead, guests and hosts are "matched" (using Tags—more on that later), which creates the opportunity for a shared experience with your host who can then choose to accept or decline. It's an inspired invitation. It's a welcome hello.

Before I go further, I want to disclose that I have been booking and casting talent in media since the 90's. First for news networks, such as CBS News, CNN, Fox News and MTV News, which ultimately led to a 10-year tenure as one of MTV's first-ever Talent Development Executives (1998–2007). I book talent for a living, and I need to be clear: PodMatch is BY FAR one of the BEST booking platforms I have ever used.

My job at MTV (1998–2007) was to source talent and develop new ways to work with them. I was lucky back then to have a hit show in the lobby of our offices, Total Request Live (TRL). TRL attracted iconic and emerging talent from all walks of life. During live shows, I would often make my way to the celebrity greenroom and make sure our guest talent knew there was an opportunity to create longform content on MTV. Access to that level of talent provided me with lifelong opportunities.

PodMatch is my new TRL. I can't name another platform that is as rich in diversity and opportunity as PodMatch.

What is one significant way that PodMatch has helped your business/mission?

Being a guest on podcasts is like getting a crash course in media training, project pitching, active listening, message refinement and talent development. Being a guest on podcasts booked through PodMatch has helped me refine my story for podcast and real-life purposes. Best of all, I now feel much more confident in bringing up topics that ultimately lead me to the desired outcomes I'm looking to inspire, impact, and ignite.

What is your daily routine in PodMatch?

I start my day by sending out a templated pitch message to matches. I focus on outbound, hopeful messaging in the morning. I focus on the energy I am inviting into my life, my schedule and my business, and then I start my day. I return at the end of the day to connect with any last matches (up to 8 a day) and use that time to respond, reply and schedule podcast interviews.

What do you recommend as the first thing a new Podcast Guest member should do after joining PodMatch?

My five steps to gaining clarity and being a successful podcast guest on PodMatch are:

1) **Gather your personal information** and promotional assets.

   - Have your website URL, social media handles and email address prepared.

   - Write a short bio (between 4–8 sentences).

   - Provide promotional photos/assets the host may use when creating promotional content for the episode. Mine includes a few variations (including transparent) of the same "press" photo, a few candid photos of me in action, and several animated gifs that I put in a google drive folder and make available to podcasters upon booking me as a guest.

2) **Identify 10 questions** you want to be asked.

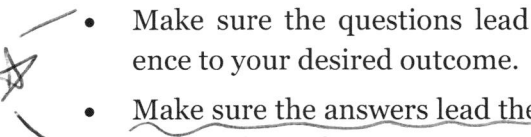

   - Make sure the questions lead the audience to your desired outcome.

   - Make sure the answers lead the audience to their desired outcome.

3) **Identify 5 topics** you want to talk about.

   - Pick topics that allow you to demonstrate your expertise.

- Pick topics that allow you to stand out.

- Pick topics that are evergreen.

4) **Pull keywords** from your **questions** and **topics** that best describe you/your expertise and use up to 10 of them as Tags in your PodMatch Guest Profile. **Tags** are crucial to the success of getting matched with podcasts as PodMatch directly utilizes the tags you enter here to match you with podcast hosts.

5) **Get clear on your call-to-action.** Most podcast hosts are not mind readers. When the host is aware of your desired outcome, it is easier to set you up for success.

What do you recommend as the second thing a new Podcast Guest member should do after joining PodMatch?

Write a templated pitch message to be used when initially connecting with a match. It's not about time-saving for me as much as it is about knowing where to start from. Mine leads off with a customizable first sentence which quickly connects to my expertise, track record, and goals. I set them up to respond in success of the info I've given, and I don't end the message with a yes or no question.

What "beginner's mistake" did you make with PodMatch that you want to warn other members about?

I waited too long to jump in. Then I didn't go through my matches daily. Then I tried to send out pitches and schedule existing opportunities all at the same time.

Now I carve out time in my week when I know I would prefer to record and prioritize the recording options that work best for my schedule.

What three PodMatch best practices should every Podcast Guest use regularly?

1) Maximize outreach to matches every day.

2) Confirm and schedule podcast D & T once a week when you have options!

3) Follow up and pin podcasts who are important to you.

What smart tip can you share for any Podcast Guest to use immediately and benefit from?

Practice! You are a guest on someone else's podcast—be respectful of the time, energy and resources they spend to make their podcast a hit! Practice, out loud, saying your name, your intro, your goals, and your stories. Use a smartphone to record your voice and get used to exercising the muscles you need to be a great articulator and communicator. Don't be afraid to speak out loud, to yourself, as you are figuring out what questions and topics you want to discuss. This is a creative rehearsal.

What smart tip can you share to help others get on podcasts where they and their message can have the most impact?

When you are crafting your message, be mindful of connecting with the audience of the podcast you are guesting on and not solely the host.

What is your final PodMatch "one thing" you want to leave readers with?

Create a *gift of gratitude.* You're the guest; be prepared to offer a way to help the host be successful in collaborating with you on this episode. Don't start with *"How can I help?"* or *"Call if you need anything."*

Don't rely on them to see what you see. Lead the conversation by asking permission to help in a way you know you can be effective. Sharing is usually a great gift of gratitude; share the episode, share a contact, share some insights or experiences. (My gift of gratitude is an invitation to be a featured podcaster on ihaveapodcast.com, more on that in the back of the book!)

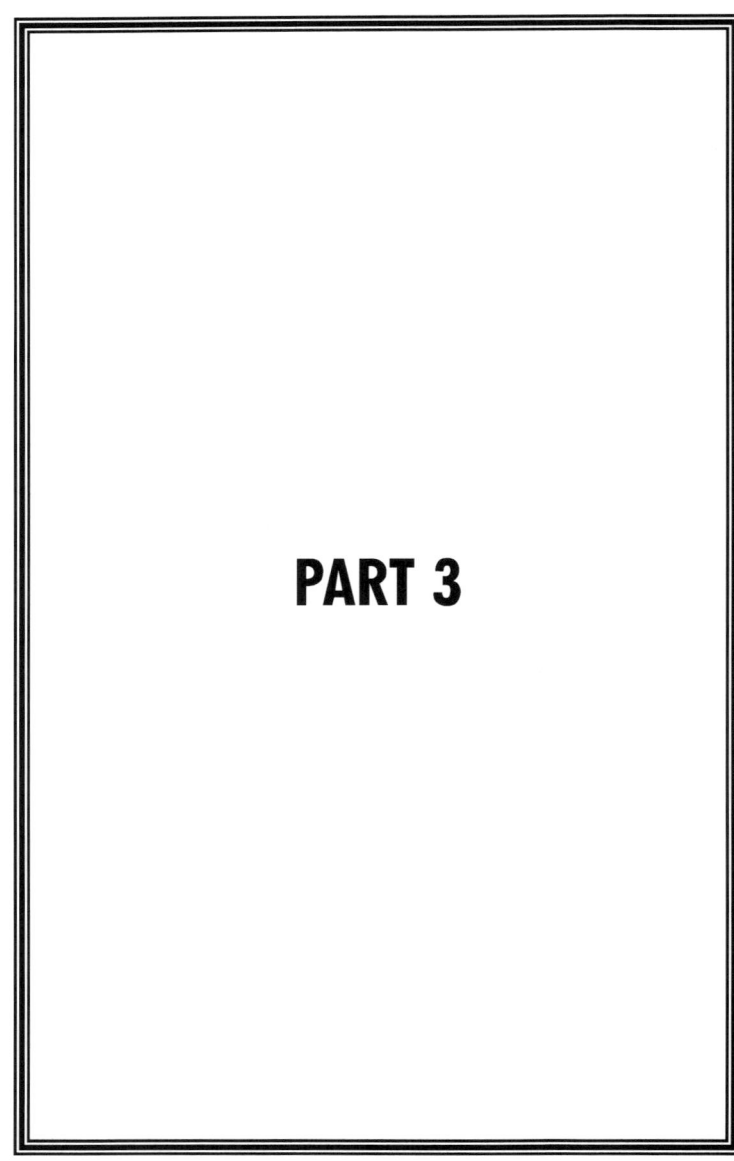

PART 3

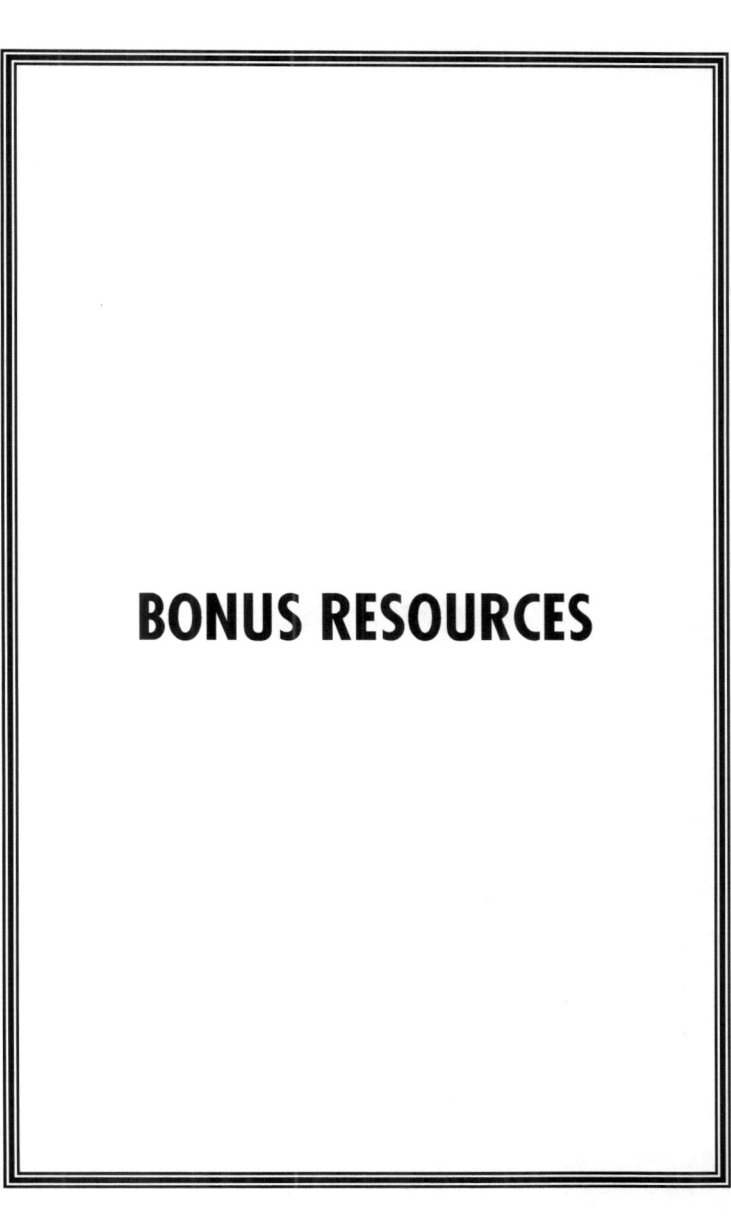

BONUS RESOURCES

GUEST ONE SHEET EXAMPLES

Podcast Guest One Sheets are an important marketing asset for any podcast guest who wants to stand out and set themself apart from other guests.

A One Sheet is exactly what it sounds like, a single page "advertisement" for you and the value you bring to a host's show. Hosts appreciate them because they give a quick overview and content necessary for the host to make you shine. Here are some ingredients of a great Guest One Sheet:

- Professionally designed.
- High-quality headshot photo.
- Short, powerful bio.
- Sample interview topics.
- Sample interview questions.
- Host testimonials.
- Contact and social media links.

Several of the guests you have met in this book included their One Sheet to inspire your own!

MIKE CAPUZZI

Key Focus: Helping Business Owners, Entrepreneurs, and Corporate Leaders Stand Out & Differentiate Themselves by Leveraging the Power of Short, Helpful Books.

ABOUT MIKE

Mike Capuzzi is an author, nonfiction book coach and short book publisher for business owners, entrepreneurs and CEOs who want to leverage the power of being a short, helpful book author.

Since 1998, Mike has helped thousands of business owners market their business smarter and since 2008, Mike has helped business owners become published authors. In 2019 he launched Bite Sized Books, a new publishing venture founded on his proven formula for creating short, helpful books (shooks™) for business owners, entrepreneurs and CEOs.

Shooks are the ideal type of book for these men and women to publish because they are easy to create, can be read in about an hour and offer helpful ways for readers to connect with the author.

Mike is the author of 15 books, including two International Amazon # 1 Best Sellers, *The 100-Page Book* and *The Magic of Short Books*.

WHAT OTHERS SAY ABOUT MIKE

- *"Mike is well versed and a great conversationalist on the topic. Motivation for anyone looking to write a "shook"! Would love to have him on again!"*
- *"Mike was a great guest and was fun to interview. Shared lots of awesome wisdom on the show."*
- *"Mike knows his stuff - highly recommended. Great conversation, clear, concise answers and stays on topic. Thank you Mike."*
- *"Mike was a great guest! Loved having him on the show. He shows up on time and prepared and engages in fun, entertaining conversation."*

SUGGESTED QUESTIONS

1. What are your three top reasons why a business owner/corporate leader should consider being a published author?
2. What a "shook" and how it is different from a traditional business book?
3. How long does it take to write a shook?
4. What is your shook "special sauce?"
5. How does one "make money" with a shook?
6. What are one or two smart shook marketing strategies?
7. I know you have gifts for my listeners. What are they and how can they get them?

ABOUT MIKE

Mike Capuzzi has been helping business owners, entrepreneurs and corporate leaders create more profitable marketing since starting his company in 1998. He is the author of 15 books, including two Amazon # 1 Best Sellers

Insightful Interviews with Business Owner Authors

ABOUT MIKE'S PODCAST

The Author Factor Podcast is focused on helping business owners, entrepreneurs and corporate leaders discover the benefits of publishing a non-fiction book. Each episode focuses on real-world tips and strategies to leverage a book to create a unique competitive advantage and grow one's business.

CONNECT WITH MIKE:

 Mike@BiteSizedBooks.com

 Facebook.com/MichaelMCapuzzi

 Linkedin.com/in/MikeCapuzziHelps

BiteSizedBooks.com MikeCapuzzi.com

TheAuthorFactor.com

https://podmatch.com/member/mike-capuzzi

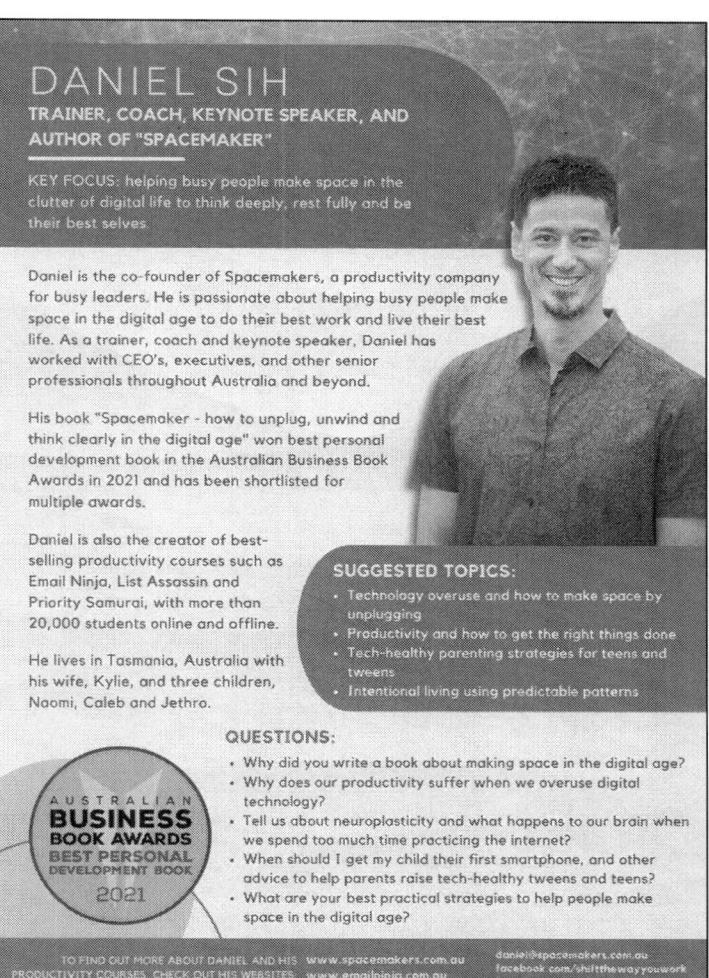

DANIEL SIH
TRAINER, COACH, KEYNOTE SPEAKER, AND AUTHOR OF "SPACEMAKER"

KEY FOCUS: helping busy people make space in the clutter of digital life to think deeply, rest fully and be their best selves.

Daniel is the co-founder of Spacemakers, a productivity company for busy leaders. He is passionate about helping busy people make space in the digital age to do their best work and live their best life. As a trainer, coach and keynote speaker, Daniel has worked with CEO's, executives, and other senior professionals throughout Australia and beyond.

His book "Spacemaker - how to unplug, unwind and think clearly in the digital age" won best personal development book in the Australian Business Book Awards in 2021 and has been shortlisted for multiple awards.

Daniel is also the creator of best-selling productivity courses such as Email Ninja, List Assassin and Priority Samurai, with more than 20,000 students online and offline.

He lives in Tasmania, Australia with his wife, Kylie, and three children, Naomi, Caleb and Jethro.

SUGGESTED TOPICS:
- Technology overuse and how to make space by unplugging
- Productivity and how to get the right things done
- Tech-healthy parenting strategies for teens and tweens
- Intentional living using predictable patterns

QUESTIONS:
- Why did you write a book about making space in the digital age?
- Why does our productivity suffer when we overuse digital technology?
- Tell us about neuroplasticity and what happens to our brain when we spend too much time practicing the internet?
- When should I get my child their first smartphone, and other advice to help parents raise tech-healthy tweens and teens?
- What are your best practical strategies to help people make space in the digital age?

AUSTRALIAN
BUSINESS
BOOK AWARDS
BEST PERSONAL
DEVELOPMENT BOOK
2021

TO FIND OUT MORE ABOUT DANIEL AND HIS PRODUCTIVITY COURSES, CHECK OUT HIS WEBSITES: www.spacemakers.com.au www.emailninja.com.au

daniel@spacemakers.com.au
facebook.com/shiftthewayyouwork
linkedin.com/in/danielsih

https://podmatch.com/member/danielsih

ANDREA PETRUT

Andrea's presence is a gift. Her ability to share hidden truths while warming people's hearts makes her a unique and powerful speaker.
- LAURI SMITH, CVO at Voice Matters, LLC

andreapetrut.ca • ap@andreapetrut.ca

Suggested Questions

1. How do we create a sustainable society for all?
2. How do we find peace and stay centered in difficult situations?
3. How do we lead with love?
4. What does servant leadership mean to you?
5. What do we need when we carve our unique path in life?
6. How can we have healthy relationships or transform the relationships we have?
7. What is important for us to know in life to make the best of the time we have to live?

Suggested Topics

1. The Power of Women Supporting Women: Lessons from a Romanian Grandmother
2. Living with Healing and Love
3. Overcoming Fear of Speaking on Stage
4. Co-empowering Empaths on a Mission to Lead and Be The Change We Want to See in The World

Biography

Andrea Petrut is a fierce advocate for love and healing, and this thread weaves through everything she does as an engaging visionary speaker, podcaster, teacher, workshop leader, trauma-informed facilitator, home educator, storyteller, somatic writer.

She is passionate about co-empowering women globally to embrace their uniqueness in order to courageously lead the change. Her warm presence encourages inspired thoughts and deeper insight that allows individuals to reach into themselves and find answers there.

As a trailblazer in her native Romanian lineage, and as an immigrant mother living in Canada, Andrea has been her own pillar in life, lifting herself and others on her path. Her goal is to guide leaders and changemakers who want to serve for the best and highest good of all. She creates holistic connection with others based on her deep belief in the oneness of all people, and is skilled at instilling collaborative energy into service ventures of all scales, from individual and community to the global level.

Featured In...

Events

- Fundraiser in partnership with Michele Noordhof (2022)
- 29+ Podcast interviews
- Host of Healing Through Oneness Podcast
- Co-Teaching Heart Imagery workshops with Margery Detring
- The Metamorphosis Summit 2022
- Becoming A Successful Immigrant Woman Fireside Chat Series (IWB - Immigrant Women in Business, 2022)
- The Healers Gather Summit 2022

An experienced speaker and facilitator, Andrea combines humour and personal stories to help your audience recognize unnecessary stress and see who they truly are. The audience will be able to begin shifting the stories that are holding them back.

https://podmatch.com/member/andreapetrut

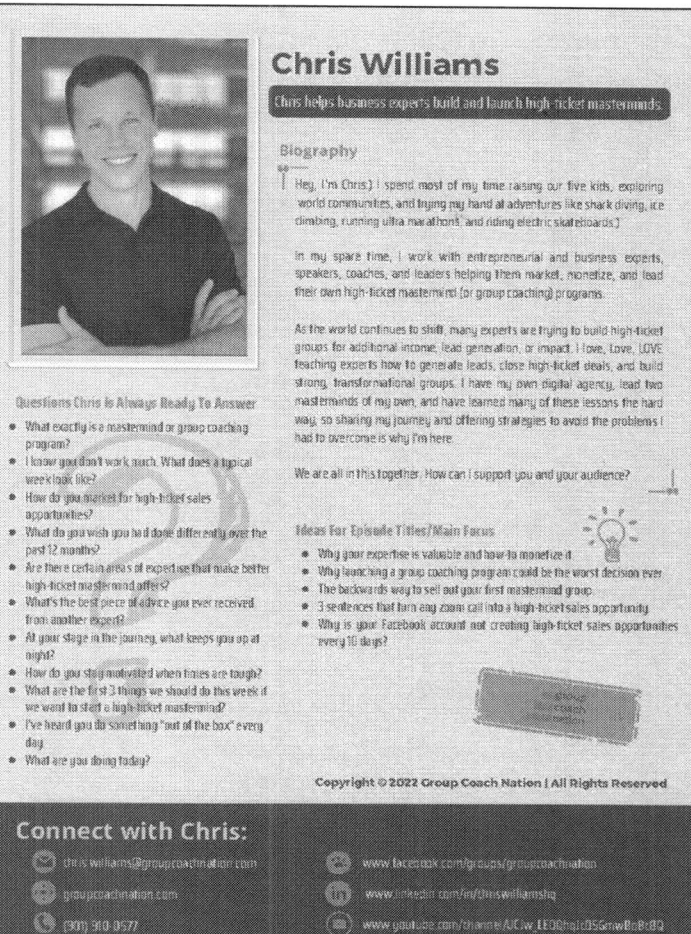

Chris Williams

Chris helps business experts build and launch high-ticket masterminds

Biography

Hey, I'm Chris! I spend most of my time raising our five kids, exploring world communities, and trying my hand at adventures like shark diving, ice climbing, running ultra marathons, and riding electric skateboards.]

In my spare time, I work with entrepreneurial and business experts, speakers, coaches, and leaders helping them market, monetize, and lead their own high-ticket mastermind (or group coaching) programs.

As the world continues to shift, many experts are trying to build high-ticket groups for additional income, lead generation, or impact. I love, love, LOVE teaching experts how to generate leads, close high-ticket deals, and build strong, transformational groups. I have my own digital agency, lead two masterminds of my own, and have learned many of these lessons the hard way, so sharing my journey and offering strategies to avoid the problems I had to overcome is why I'm here.

We are all in this together. How can I support you and your audience?

Questions Chris Is Always Ready To Answer

- What exactly is a mastermind or group coaching program?
- I know you don't work much. What does a typical week look like?
- How do you market for high-ticket sales opportunities?
- What do you wish you had done differently over the past 12 months?
- Are there certain areas of expertise that make better high-ticket mastermind offers?
- What's the best piece of advice you ever received from another expert?
- At your stage in the journey, what keeps you up at night?
- How do you stay motivated when times are tough?
- What are the first 3 things we should do this week if we want to start a high-ticket mastermind?
- I've heard you do something "out of the box" every day.
- What are you doing today?

Ideas For Episode Titles/Main Focus

- Why your expertise is valuable and how to monetize it
- Why launching a group coaching program could be the worst decision ever
- The backwards way to sell out your first mastermind group
- 3 sentences that turn any zoom call into a high-ticket sales opportunity
- Why is your Facebook account not creating high-ticket sales opportunities every 10 days?

Connect with Chris:

- chris.williams@groupcoachnation.com
- groupcoachnation.com
- (901) 910-0577
- www.facebook.com/chris.williamshq
- www.facebook.com/groups/groupcoachnation
- www.linkedin.com/in/chriswilliamshq
- www.youtube.com/channel/UCjw_EE0GhqIc0SGmwBoBcBQ
- www.instagram.com/chriswilliamshq

https://podmatch.com/member/chris-williams

https://podmatch.com/member/tylerfoley

MICHAEL HARRIS

"Igniting the power of compelling stories to change the world."

Topics Michael is ready to speak on at anytime.

Quantum Leaps, Take One Anytime
An in-depth look at when to take small steps and when to take quantum leaps.

Disconnect the Monkey Mind
A new view of mindset and what anyone can do to quiet the fluctuations of the mind for more focused performance at work and home.

Life as an Entrepreneur
How childhood teaches us everything needed to know about blazing our own trail.

Biography
Michael is an entrepreneur, dynamic business coach, #1 bestselling author, remarkable storyteller, yoga teacher and is dedicated to helping others get their voice, message and story out to the world with a bit of fun and pizazz.

Offerings
Keynote Address - Tailored to your specific event with your audiences challenges & solutions in mind.
Workshops – Choose from various topics including The Quantum Leap Framework, Accelerated Podcast Guesting, Business Functions Mastery, and more.

Michael as seen on...

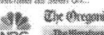 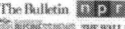

"Michael is an excellent speaker, with a lot of knowledge that he is sharing in a very interactive way. Very grateful to have had him on my show." Diana Poppa

"I've had the pleasure to hear Michael speak a number of times. Each time I am amazed how much more I learn about myself." Jonalyn Henie

Michael is the #1 bestselling author of "Falling Down Getting UP"
Foreword by Jay Conrad Levinson – Father of Guerrilla Marketing

See Michael's Complete Bio's & Images:
https://www.michaelbharris.com/approved-media
See Michael's PodMatch Profile:
https://podmatch.com/member/michaelharris

https://podmatch.com/member/michaelharris

WADE GALT

Founder of 3-Day Weekend Club
Host of the 3-Day Weekend Entrepreneur Podcast

I can help your audience **Create a Meaningful Life** & **Profitable Business** while **Doing Work they Enjoy** & Believe In.

- Create Time for the Most Important Relationships & Activities in Their Life
- Increase Income, While Reducing Work Time
- Focus on Their Highest Impact / Highest Income Projects & Eliminate, Delegate or Automate the Rest
- Optimize the Relationships, Time, Money, & Things already in Their Life.

It took me 7 years after graduating college to start my own business, & 15 more years to create an abundant & sustainable 3-Day Weekend Lifestyle. I can help your listeners (and you, if you like) do this much quicker. You & your audience will learn actionable wisdom & strategies to create better life / work harmony and live a life you truly enjoy.

I will share our episode through all my social media, with my 10k+ Udemy students, and with my email list.

Best Topics:

- Create a 3-Day Weekend Lifestyle in Under 12 Months
- Create the Time for the Most Important People & Activities in Your Life
- How to Decrease Your Work Hours 20% & Make 20% More Income in 90 Days
- Create More Energy & Fun in Life by Doing Work You Love
- Align Your Body, Heart, Mind, and Spirit to Create Greater Impact & Income

Potential Questions:

1. Should people **do what they love** for living or do their soul work as a hobby?
2. Why do so many financially rich people fail to **make time to enjoy life**?
3. What's the best way to start **profitably delegating tasks**?
4. **How long should it take** to create a sustainable 3-Day Weekend Lifestyle?
5. How can I best **align my spiritual & family values** with my work?
6. How can **employees negotiate a 3-Day Weekend Lifestyle** agreement at work?
7. What's the simplest way to **attract, motivate, afford & keep great employees**?
8. What's the most effective way to **build a team of high-quality freelancers**?
9. How do I know when it's time to **scale & grow my business**?
10. How can I filter & **attract my most ideal clients** without wasting my time?

Gift for the Audience

3-Day Weekend Club
Community Membership

About Wade

Wade teaches Entrepreneurs & Professionals to create an abundant & sustainable 3-Day Weekend lifestyle so they can better enjoy their family, friends, and life.

He's a 20+ year Software Company Founder, Business Growth Coach and Author of books on business growth, personal growth, parenting, & spirituality.

He & his family have lived ocean-side in North & South America.

He enjoys 3-day weekends and Fridays at the beach playing volleyball with friends + weekends with his family.

- 3dayweekendclub.com
- Podcast
- wadegalt
- wadegalt.com
- 3dayweekendentrepreneur
- 3dayweekendentrepreneur
- 3dayweekendentrepreneur
- 3dayweekendentrepreneur

https://podmatch.com/member/wadegalt

Mission - helping leaders communicate more consciously, creating teams of engaged and thriving people.

Jem is an executive leadership coach, best selling author, international retreat facilitator and TEDx speaker. He draws on his decades of extreme, global experiences, cross-cultural connections and corporate consulting to teach leaders more conscious and effective ways to communicate. Jem's online courses in Resilience, Mindfulness, Emotional Management and Communication, have been endorsed by government bodies and achieved critical and professional acclaim. His book, The Art of Conscious Communication for Thoughtful Men, delivers clear and straight-forward strategies to immediately elevate your ability to communicate, and fulfil your potential in all areas of life that matter to you.

JEM FULLER

Suggested Questions

1. Why is communication important?
2. What gets in the way of communication?
3. How does better communication help leaders?
4. Are there processes you've designed to help communication?
5. What is 'conscious communication'?
6. Where does conscious communication begin?

Suggested Topics

1. How do people with different points of view communicate?
2. Is it too late for humans to learn better communication?
3. How ego gets in the way
4. The quality of our relationships determines the quality of our lives

CONNECT WITH JEM

hello@jemfuller.com

www.jemfuller.com

+61 412 484 448

https://podmatch.com/member/jemfuller

GUEST ONE SHEET EXAMPLES

John Lee and Mark X. Cronin

Podcast Guests - Entrepreneurs – Speakers – Philanthropists - Inspirations

John Cronin and his Dad, Mark X. Cronin are the co-founders of John's Crazy Socks, a social enterprise with a mission to spread happiness. In five years, they bootstrapped their start up into the world's largest sock store with multi-million-dollar sales in 88 nations. John may have Down syndrome, but he always says, "Down syndrome never holds me back."

More than half our employees have a differing ability and every day, John & Mark show what their colleagues can do. They are fierce advocates for the rights of the differently abled and have testified twice before the U.S. Congress and spoken at the United Nations and recorded two TEDx Talks.

John and Mark are winners of the EY Entrepreneur of the Year and the Monsignor Thomas J. Hartman Humanitarian of the Year Award. They have addressed audiences across the U.S., Canada and Mexico speaking before social service agencies, fundraisers, universities, and corporations (e.g., Microsoft, EY & Bank of America). As experienced podcast guests, they will delight your audience.

John's Crazy Socks is Built on 5 Pillars:

Inspiration and hope: Hiring and showing what people with differing abilities can do.

Giving Back: 5% of earnings go to the Special Olympics, plus their Awareness Socks raise money for charity partners.

Socks You Will Love: Over 4,000 choices makes John's Crazy Socks the world's largest sock store.

Making It Personal: Every package gets a thank you note from John and candy.

Make It a Great Place to Work: Create a workplace our colleagues can love.

John & Mark Make Great Podcast Guests:

Experienced and professional performers

Ability to share your podcast on our website and social media platforms (245,000 FB followers)

Offer promo code for your listeners

Professional set up (microphone, camera, lighting)

We will provide bios, photos and support material to make John and Mark's appearance on your podcast easy for you.

Please call us at 631-760-5625 or email Maria at podcast@johnscrazysocks.com
JohnsCrazySocks.com

https://podmatch.com/member/markxcronin

150

Amy Scruggs is known in country music for more than 15 years opening for greats including Clint Black, Trace Adkins, Charlies and many more. She was the spokesperson for the American Veterans of California (AMVETS) 2009-2011.

Amy's career also includes 20 years in sales team coaching and received Bestseller on her book "Lights Camera Action" in 2021. The past 5 years she enjoyed her position as TV Host for The American Dream TV on CNBC and several other shows.

Amy uses her experience as a Media Executive, TV host, Recording Artist, and Public Speaker to help others communicate a concise and professional message for network TV, podcast, social media or in person public speaking appearances.

Her new single released in 2022, "What if it All Goes Right" is on radio worldwide including reaching #66 on the Music Row Charts along with being selected for the NY Times Summer 2022 Playlist.

Topics Include

- Self-Awareness
- The Art Of Messaging
- First Impressions
- Virtual Meetings And Webinars
- Mastering Your Comfort on Camera
- Proper Posture and Attire
- Proper Equipment
- Effective Communication
- Preparation & Training
- Putting It All Together

AMY SCRUGGS MEDIA

www.amyscruggsmedia.com

info@amyscruggsmedia.com
facebook.com/amyscruggstvhost
Spotify/AmyScruggs
Instagram amyscruggsmedia

https://podmatch.com/member/amyscruggs

Daniel Alfon
LinkedIn Author • Speaker • Trainer

Speaker one sheet

Helping you get results organically
- Without spending $10K on ads
- Without sharing to death
- Without spamming your network

Most popular talks
- Starting a Business
- Podcasting
- $ Getting clients as a consultant

Bio

Daniel Alfon is the author of *Build a LinkedIn Profile for Business Success*.

Daniel joined LinkedIn in early 2004 and publishes Articles, interviews and exclusive content about advanced LinkedIn strategies to clients and subscribers on his website, www.danielalfon.com.

Find Daniel Alfon:

Contact: nfo@DanielAlfon.com

https://podmatch.com/member/alfon

Peter George

Public Speaking Coach, Speaker, Author
Peter George Public Speaking, Inc.
"be calm, confident, and credible®"

contact
Peter@PeterGeorgePublicSpeaking.com
+1 401-742-1231

quick overview
- public speaking coach (17 years)
- public speaker (35 years)
- author of *The Captivating Public Speaker: Engage, Impact, and Inspire Your Audience Every Time*
- creator of the AMP'D Framework™
- TEDx coach
- host of the *Public Speaking with Peter George* podcast

bio (feel free to edit)
Peter believes that everyone should be able to confidently share their knowledge and experience.

As a public speaking coach, he specializes in helping professional speakers, authors, consultants, and executives be calm, confident, and credible® every time they speak.

Throughout his childhood, Peter dealt with a lisp and a stutter. Consequently, he grew up shy and introverted, avoiding communicating with others as much as possible.

When he got into the business world, he quickly realized that his lack of presentation skills kept him at a disadvantage. After seeking help, he now credits his public speaking coaches for much of his business success.

Over the past 17 years, Peter has helped professionals from around the corner to those in Fortune 100 companies develop into speakers who understand how to craft and deliver presentations that engage, persuade, and inspire, ultimately helping them increase their impact, influence, and income.

Peter is the host of the *Public Speaking with Peter George* podcast.

His book, *The Captivating Public Speaker: Engage, Impact, and Inspire Your Audience Every Time*, is available on Amazon.

book
The Captivating Public Speaker: Engage, Impact, and Inspire Your Audience Every Time

podcast
Public Speaking with Peter George

free resource for listeners
52 Free Public Speaking Tips. Available at PeterGeorgePublicSpeaking.com/tips/

links for resource section

website	*book on amazon*	*linkedin*
PeterGeorgePublicSpeaking.com	https://amzn.to/3vsfUss	https://www.linkedin.com/in/petergeorgepublicspeaking/

PeterGeorgePublicSpeaking.com
Peter@PeterGeorgePublicSpeaking.com
+1-401-742-1231

https://podmatch.com/member/petergeorge

HELPING PERSONAL BRANDS EVOLVE THROUGH PODCASTS SINCE 2015

QUICK BIO (for podcast intros)

Jason Cercone is a personal brand architect, creator, and podcaster. He helps entrepreneurs, leaders, and professionals leverage the brand-building power of the podcast medium to establish authority, increase visibility, and accelerate the evolution of their personal brand. He also hosts Evolution of Brand, a podcast featuring authentic entrepreneurs and professionals sharing inspirational stories and tactical brand-building strategies to help you succeed in your professional pursuits.

MY BRAND EVOLUTION

The entrepreneurial bug bit me when I started flipping sports cards to friends and at local collectors shows when I was just 13 years old and I never looked back. The path has most definitely been winding - filled with obstacles, pivots, and the unexpected loss of my last corporate job. But throughout that time, I've also experienced growth, evolution, victories, and the privilege of partnering and collaborating with like-minded professionals who share my passions and beliefs.

QUICK FACTS

- Jason has been podcasting since 2015
- Currently hosts Evolution of Brand
- 900+ lifetime combined podcast appearances and episodes produced
- Over 20 years in sales, marketing, content creation, and brand management
- Believes the podcast medium is the best stage for networking and personal brand development

CHECK OUT MY PODCAST APPEARANCES
IMAGE GALLERY
EMAIL ME FOR ALL GUEST INQUIRIES
QUESTIONS? CALL ME AT 412.965.8428

KEY FOCUS TOPICS

- How to establish authority, increase visibility, and accelerate personal brand growth as a podcast guest
- Why podcasts are the world's greatest digital networking platform
- Starting your own podcast vs. Guesting on established podcasts - which one is better for your brand?
- The game-changing benefits of being a confident, compelling podcast guest
- How to sell your products, services, and offers on podcasts without actually selling

CONVERSATION STARTERS

- Why should entrepreneurs and professionals in all niches utilize the podcast platform to build their personal brand?
- What are some of the important benefits to building your personal brand in the podcast space?
- How do speaking skills developed and utilized on podcasts translate to other areas of your life?
- Do you need your own podcast in order to maximize ROI on the podcast platform?
- What are some aspects of podcast guesting where people drop the ball?
- What is the most powerful benefit of podcasting that many, many people overlook and ignore?
- Why do most guest pitches, presentations, and outreach strategies suck?
- Why is it imperative that podcast guests close their interview with a Unique Call to Action that points to their website?
- What is the fastest way to improve your podcast?
- Why are download numbers a skewed vanity metric?

HIGH PRAISE

"Jason is what I would call a Platinum Podcast Guest. He put together a great idea for a collaborative interview, showed up on time, had great technology, and didn't leave anything on the table. If you're looking for a guest who will truly bring value to your audience, this is the guy. I typically say no to 98% of the pitches I get for guests. But Jason's preparation and pitch blew my mind! It was a no-brainer addition to my content." --- Travis Brown, Founder of Social Boom and Content Creator Club

https://podmatch.com/member/jasoncercone

https://podmatch.com/member/vinniepotestivo

Steve Lowell

Master Trainer To High-Impact Speakers

Steve Lowell is a multi-award-winning speaker, 3x #1 best-selling author, and master trainer for high-impact speakers with a track record that speaks for itself. Having given over 3500 keynote speeches, 5000 seminars and trained more than 500K speakers globally, Steve delivers innovative strategies that help speakers drive revenue from the stage and build wealth through speaking.

Steve is the Past President of the Global Speakers Federation (GSF) and the Past National President of the Canadian Association of Professional Speakers (CAPS). With over 50 years on stage (Steve started speaking at the age of 6!), thousands trained, and unmatched results, Steve helps speakers craft their signature transformational message and turn it into revenue.

Most Requested Topics:

- How To Be A Transformational Speaker
- The Three Circles Of Speaking Energy
- How To Monetize Your Message With Speaking
- Speak to Sell...Without Selling

Suggested Questions:

- How does an entrepreneur make money when they speak?
- What makes someone a "transformational" speaker instead of just a speaker?
- Can anyone be a good speaker or does it take some special skills?
- What's the best way to earn a living as a speaker?
- What's the secret to selling from the stage when selling from the stage is not allowed?

Here's What They're Saying

"Steve Lowell is one of the best trainers and teachers in the world today"
- Brian Tracy, Legendary Business Speaker and Guru

"If you're thinking of working with Steve, run don't walk...it will be an amazing experience I promise you!"
- Jack Canfield, Co-Author, Chicken Soup for the Soul

"I'm so impressed with the work Steve Lowell is doing all over the world"
- Kevin Harrington, Original shark on "Shark Tank", creator of "As Seen on TV"

Quick Facts

- Founder, The High-Impact Speaker's Studio
- 2021 Past-President Global Speakers Federation
- 3x #1 International Best Selling Author
- 2020 Author Of The Year, Hasmark Publishing
- 2019 Speaker Of The Year, PSA, UK
- 2018 President, Canadian Association of Professional Speakers
- Certified Speaking Professional, National Speakers Association

Connect With Steve

www.SteveLowell.com

- facebook.com/HighImpactSpeakers
- twitter.com/SteveLowell
- instagram.com/TheRealSteveLowell
- youtube.com/SteveLowell
- linkedin.com/in/SteveLowell

For requests for appearances, including JV or affiliate opportunities, media inquiries, or publicity, reach out to Jayne Lowell.

- Jayne@SteveLowell.com
- 514-953-6317

https://podmatch.com/member/stevelowell

GIFTS FOR READERS

To further increase the value and impact of this book, we asked members to offer a valuable gift for readers to help them with their podcast guesting journey. We hope you enjoy and profit from these gifts.

Mike Capuzzi's gift:

I help business owners, entrepreneurs and corporate leaders write and publish short, helpful books that are quick to read and easy to publish. I am offering readers of PodMatch Guest Mastery the opportunity to get my *Short Book Magic Kit*, which includes three valuable books, including my Amazon #1 best selling book, *The Magic of Short Books*. Visit:

https://MikeCapuzzi.com/podmatch-books

Daniel Sih's gift:

I'm thrilled to invite you to download free chapters of my award-winning book, *Spacemaker*, to help you make space across your work and life. You will also receive a practical worksheet and videos to help you design a weekly day of rest, also known as a digital sabbath. Visit:

https://Spacemakers.com.au/book

Andrea Petrut's gift:

Podcast guesting is a journey and each guest has a unique one, especially when you are a one-of-a-kind love rebel on a mission. Get access to exclusive insights and nuggets from Andrea's experience as she's leading her way purposefully and strategically to inspire and succeed on her path.

https://AndreaPetrut.ca/podmatchbookbonus

Tonya Eberhart & Michael Carr's gift:

Want to know how to attract more, convert more, and charge more for your services while spending less on marketing? Download our FREE guide and learn how to build an outstanding personal brand:

https://BrandFaceforExperts.com/guide

Chris Williams' gift:

I created a checklist, an illustrative flowchart, and full video walk-through with everything you need so you can begin monetizing your podcast appearances by using PodMatch. To download your free checklist, flowchart, and watch the full video walk-through, visit:

https://PodMatchlm.GroupCoachNation.com/ monetize-podcast-guesting

Tyler Foley's gift:

Want to improve your public speaking skills or become a more engaging and persuasive speaker? Then the Ultimate Speaker Kit is for you. This comprehensive collection includes my most used tools and resources, to capture your audience's attention, deliver your message with confidence, and use storytelling to enhance your impact.

http://EndlessStages.com/ultimate-speaker

Michael Harris' gift:

Get The Ultimate Guide to Being an Outrageously Great Podcast Guest, so you can quickly attract new raving fans, build your business and make your mark on the world. Visit:

http://EndlessStages.com/pod-guide

Wade Galt's gift:

Get the 3-Day Weekend Club Membership + Game Plan Course. Design the strategy to create your 3-Day Weekend Lifestyle + get support implementing it. It includes a free online course + coaching member community.

https://3DayWeekendClub.com

Jem Fuller's gift:

Mindfulness Meditation is a practice that brings more ease, perspective and happiness to life. To make it easier for people to understand and implement, Jem designed and recorded his Mindfulness Made Easy, and he would like to gift it to you for free. Visit this website and enter coupon code SPRINGGIFT:

https://JemFuller.Teachable.com

Steve Lowell's gift:

Download the "Transformational Content Check-list" and discover what it takes to be a truly transformational speaker. Be the one who everyone remembers! Visit:

https://SpeakerContentChecklist.com

John & Mark Cronin's gift:

We want to thank PodMatch supporters by offering a 10% discount on your next order. Just use the code *PodMatch10* at:

https://JohnsCrazySocks.com

Amy Scruggs' gift:

Amy Scruggs Media Coaching is offering 50% off the "Media Coaching Course for Professionals." This complete course is available online and will allow you to go through the modules at your own pace to help prepare you for your podcast guest success. Use promo code PODMATCH at checkout:

https://AmyScruggsMedia.com

Peter George's gift:

Do you want to be calm, confident, and credible® every time you speak? Then get your Free Weekly Public Speaking Tips at:

https://PeterGeorgePublicSpeaking.com/tips

Jason Cercone's gift:

Want to maximize the ROI on your podcast guest appearances? Check out my Guest Accelerator program. Mention this book and receive a $150 credit towards either level of training! Discover how to take your guesting efforts to the next level. Visit:

http://GuestAccelerator.com

Vinnie Potestivo's gift:

Now is your chance to get discovered! All Pod-Match guests and hosts are welcome to apply. To claim your FREE Featured Podcaster Article and get featured on Google News go to:

https://ihaveapodcast.com/interview

NOT A PODMATCH MEMBER YET?

PodMatch is the premier site for entrepreneurs, thought leaders and influencers to find some of the world's top podcast shows and be a featured guest.

With two value-packed membership levels, joining PodMatch is one of the smartest and most cost-effective ways to share your message on other pod-cast shows.

Joining the PodMatch family is quick and simple. Just visit:

https://podmatch.com/signup/today

Made in the USA
Columbia, SC
24 March 2023

14215100R00098